Cool Pose

The Dilemmas of Black Manhood in America

Richard Majors

Janet Mancini Billson

A TOUCHSTONE BOOK
Published by Simon & Schuster
New York   London   Toronto
Sydney   Tokyo   Singapore

TOUCHSTONE

Rockefeller Center
1230 Avenue of the Americas
New York, New York 10020

Copyright © 1992 by Lexington Books
An Imprint of Macmillan, Inc.

First Touchstone Edition 1993
Published by arrangement with Lexington Books,
an imprint of Macmillan, Inc.
TOUCHSTONE and colophon are registered trademarks
of Simon & Schuster Inc.
Manufactured in the United States of America

5   7   9   10   8   6   4

Library of Congress Cataloging-in-Publication Data
Majors, Richard.
Cool pose : the dilemmas of black manhood in America /
Richard Majors. Janet Mancini Billson.—
1st Touchstone ed.
p.   cm.
Originally published: New York : Lexington, © 1992.
"A Touchstone book."
Includes bibliographical references (p.) and index.
1. Afro-American man.
I. Billson, Janet Mancini.   II. Title.
[E185.86.M35   1993]
305.38′896073—dc20   93-989
                                                                        CIP
ISBN: 0-671-86572-2

For my grandmother,
Lillian Amy McGill:
Your love
and nurturing
made possible
all that I feel and do.
RM

For my children,
Mark and Kyra Mancini,
and for all the children.
JMB

Contents

8 Playing the Dozens   91

9 Summary and Implications   105

Preface

This is a book for young black males in America. It is for their parents, their wives and lovers, their teachers, neighbors, and friends. It is for those who seek insight into how a sense of self is created in the face of daily insults and oppression. It is for those who stand in awe of the powerful cultural statement that black males make when they are cool. And it is for those who find themselves frustrated by the mask of cool that hides deeper vulnerabilities.

Being cool, or adopting a cool pose as we call it, is a strategy that many black males use in making sense of their everyday lives. We believe that coolness as a strength may be linked to pride, self-respect, and masculinity. At the same time, coolness as a mask may contribute to dropping out of school, getting into trouble, sliding into drug and alcohol abuse, and being sucked into delinquent or criminal street gangs.

Cool pose may be a factor in frustrating love relationships and violence in the home and on the streets. As a response to a history of oppression and social isolation in this country, coolness may be a survival strategy that has cost the black male—and society—an enormous price.

Although most people in the African-American community have an intuitive sense of what it means to be cool, this important form of self-expression has been difficult to pin down through traditional social science research methods. Therefore, we have gone to those who are the experts on cool pose—young black males—in order to try to capture its emotional and cultural significance.

We have incorporated the best scholarship on African-American males, past and present, into this book; yet, it remains descriptive and introspective in nature. Our hypothesis regarding the positive and negative aspects of being cool should be viewed as speculative and exploratory. It is only one way to enter the complicated world of African-American males and the special dilemmas they have faced for centuries.

We stress that cool pose—which certainly characterizes the style of *some* black males, some of the time—does not apply to all black males, all of the time. Cool pose is a strategy *available* for use in the black community but is only one of many coping strategies developed within the American context. To overstate our case or to assume that cool pose is common to *all* black males would be both inaccurate and counterproductive. Our exploration of cool pose is intended to enrich our understandings, not to furnish stereotypes.

We are concerned with how some black males use coolness to counter the stresses of oppression, but cool pose is not necessarily dependent on poverty, unemployment, or ghetto living. People of all racial, ethnic, class, and gender groups use cool behaviors to some extent. However, because of the legacy of slavery and because black males in the United States have been subjected to systematic discrimination and unusually harsh conditions, we suspect cool behaviors have emerged with more frequency and intensity among low income black males than in other groups.

We believe that those who come into daily contact with the dreams, both shattered and fulfilled, of young black males will benefit from a more complex view of black masculinity. We hope this book will encourage further research on coolness. And we hope that our elaboration of the causes and consequences of cool will stimulate discussion in the African-American community.

Acknowledgments

The voices of young black men (and a few women) are heard throughout these pages. They are telling it "like it is" in the color and creativity of their own words. We wish to pay tribute to the youths whose lives, one way or another, have contributed to our understanding of cool pose. The list includes those who have participated in studies by other social scientists, written about their own lives, or assisted us directly in the writing of this book.

A central voice is that of "Phil," who opened up his mind and his world through hours of intensive conversations with Richard Majors. Majors initially met Phil through informal contacts in elevators and halls of a building where both worked. Phil, an authentic streetman living in a poor section of a mid-western black community, had experienced difficulties with white authority figures and had encountered drugs and alcohol problems. He was willing to share his experiences during long hours of interviewing. Phil's honesty and sincerity provided the insights essential to the process of defining cool pose and its meaning for black males.*

Other voices are heard in the interleaves between chapters; they were taped in rap sessions conducted in early 1991 by Charles Martinez, Providence firefighter, who organized brothers and sisters into discussions of the meaning and many faces of cool. We wish to extend our appreciation to him and to Robert Wuelleh, Hillary Johnson, Paul Alex Stacks, Tara Colbert, Obed Hoyah, Tina Smith, and Angel Corprew for their honesty and sincere participation.

*The interviews with Phil provided the central experiential data for Majors' doctoral dissertation, "Cool pose: A new approach toward a systematic understanding and study of Black male behavior," which he completed at the University of Illinois, Urbana-Champaign, in 1987. It is available through University Microfilms International, Ann Arbor, Michigan.

Their comments have been disguised under pseudonyms, but the ages remain similar.

The voices of the Pathways boys, especially "Leroy," are also heard throughout these pages. Together with quotations from research conducted by others found in the bibliography, they enrich our understanding of cool pose.

Like most books, this one is the result of collaboration and support from many people. We both wish to acknowledge the expertise of the editorial staff at Lexington Books in bringing the book from conception to completion. Their professionalism and commitment to the project have enhanced our efforts. We extend our gratitude especially to our editor, Margaret Zusky, and to Andrea Martin.

For her meticulous typing of the original manuscript, we thank Kyra Mancini, research assistant *par excellence*. John C. Kortenbeutel, Charles Allsworth, and Norman T. London rendered important photographic support.

Richard Majors

I am indebted to many people whose help, support, and advice have been invaluable in writing this book. First, let me thank the late J. McVicker Hunt for his loving support, intellectual feedback, and unwavering confidence in me.

Many friends and family members have contributed directly or indirectly: Viola Scott, who took me under her wing when my grandmother passed away; my best friends, Eugene Scott, Charles Hughes, Glenn Martin, and Greg Foster; for their spiritual support and guidance, Klaus Witz, Mario Anderson, Ron Hall, Sandy Parker, Tara Huebner, the late Sakari Sariola, Philip Jones, Robert Sprague, the late Dr. Stuart Jones, and my "spiritual guru," Vera Mitchell. For their advice and support, I thank Norman Denzin, Steve Tozier, Harry Triandis, Terry Denny, John Ogbu, Ralph Page, Ken Monterio, Elaine Copeland, and Helen Farmer. Special thanks are due to Klaus Witz and Jack Easley for allowing me the time and freedom to develop the original research on cool pose in a creative fashion.

Finally, I wish to express my appreciation to the American Psychological Association for funding my research on cool pose with a Predoctoral Minority Fellowship Research Award.

Janet Mancini Billson

For the inspiration and opportunity to participate in Harvard's *Pathways to Identity* project in the 1960s and 1970s, I am indebted to Robert A. Rosenthal, Bernard E. Bruce, Florence Shelton Ladd, and Barbara L. Carter. As the young black males living in Roxbury at that time clearly reported, being cool was a central part of their identity. I wrote the chapter on "the cool guy" in *Strategic Styles: Coping in the Inner City* (1981) after sifting through hundreds of hours of interviews conducted by same-sex, same-race members of the community and with invaluable guidance from the Pathways staff.

A decade later, it is time to devote an entire book to being cool. I am grateful for generous gifts of released time from Rhode Island College for its preparation. And I am deeply appreciative of the support of my colleagues, friends, and family throughout the arduous process of trying to do justice to the lives and words of others.

Special thanks go to my husband, Norman London, for helping construct a peaceful atmosphere conducive to writing, and for being there in every way.

To be cool is to throw off an air like nothing can hurt you. Confident. That's the only label they can cling to, that the white man can't take away.

—*Sandy, 25*

A cool person basically doesn't go by trends. He's basically like himself all the time. He has goals, working toward them, and he's not being sidetracked. Being cool is like being honest to yourself. I'm like this today and I'm going to act the same way tomorrow. It's uncool to try to act cool.

—*Wayne, 23*

A cool person is someone who is out for what their goals are: this is what I want in five to ten years. It's not just listening to a group of people.

—*Sandy, 25*

If you give the impression that you're confident, you give the air that you can't be touched, you can't be damaged. No black man in our society wants to seem vulnerable. But a lot of times this coolness is used in the wrong manner. Some people are more confident in themselves than those that need to give a false air of confidence. But you can usually tell who is really confident. They have goals, they're respectful towards themselves and they respect other people. They have a vision to achieve those goals.

—*Trish, 31*

1

Cool Pose

Expression and Survival

I play it cool
And dig all jive,
That's the reason
I stay alive.
My motto as I live and learn
is: Dig and be dug in return.
—*Langston Hughes*

Being cool is not a way of life for teenagers, it is life . . .
—*Stanlaw and Peshkin*

Historically, racism and discrimination have inflicted a variety of harsh injustices on African-Americans in the United States, especially on males. Being male and black has meant being psychologically castrated—rendered impotent in the economic, political, and social arenas that whites have historically dominated. Black men learned long ago that the classic American virtues of thrift, perseverance, and hard work did not give them the same tangible rewards that accrued to whites.

Yet African-American men have defined manhood in terms familiar to white men: breadwinner, provider, procreator, protector. Unlike white men, however, blacks have not had consistent access to the same means to fulfill their dreams of masculinity and success. Many have become frustrated, angry, embittered, alienated, and impatient. Some have learned to mistrust the words and actions of the dominant culture.

This book is about how black males, especially those who are young and live in the inner cities of our nation, have adopted and used cool masculinity—or as we prefer to call it, "cool pose"—as a way of surviving in a restrictive society. It is about how black males have created a tool for hammering masculinity out of the bronze of their daily lives. And it is about how cool pose propels black males on a collision course with each other and with whites.

Some African-American males have channeled their creative energies into the construction of a symbolic universe. Denied access to mainstream avenues of success, they have created their own voice. Unique patterns of speech, walk, and demeanor express the cool pose.[1] This strategic style allows the black male to tip society's imbalanced scales in his favor. Coolness means poise under pressure and the ability to maintain detachment, even during tense encounters. Being cool invigorates a life that would otherwise be degrading and empty. It helps the black male make sense out of his life and get what he wants from others. Cool pose brings a dynamic vitality into the black male's everyday encounters, transforming the mundane into the sublime and making the routine spectacular.

The Dilemmas of Black Masculinity

Striving for masculinity presents dilemmas for the black male because it is so often grounded in masking strategies that rest on denial and suppression of deep feelings. On the one hand, cool pose embodies the kaleidoscopic brilliance of the black male self. People are drawn to the power of the cool black male because he epitomizes control, strength, and pride. He presents a mysterious challenge. He is charismatic, suave, debonair, entertaining.

On the other hand, being cool can become more important than life itself. Unfortunately, it can exact a price that seems destructively high. We believe that cool pose helps to explain the fact that African-American males die earlier and faster than white males from suicide, homicide, accidents, and stress-related illnesses; that black males are more deeply involved in criminal and delinquent activities; that they drop out of school and are suspended more often than white children; and that they have more volatile relationships with women. Cool pose is implicated in the fact that, as Gibbs and others have noted in the 1980s, the young black male in America is an endangered species.

In this book, we take a close look at two basic questions: How does cool pose help bring balance, stability, confidence, and a sense of masculinity to those African-American males who adopt it, and how does cool pose work destructively in their lives?

With few exceptions, the systematic study of cool has virtually been ignored. Because social scientists tend to perceive cool as a colloquial term—and because they do not view cool as a coping mechanism—the research tends to be more descriptive than analytical. Coolness has not been examined as a universal phenomenon that cuts across race, gender, and class, although it is certainly utilized by humans around the world. Nor has cool behavior been explored as a critical psychological defense used by some black males to ward off the ill effects of racial oppression and social inequality, although it certainly has been significant since the days of slavery in America.

In our book, we show the historical, social, and cultural significance of cool in the lives of some African-American males. We explore how some black males, especially those who live in lower economic circumstances, use cool behavior as an expressive performance that helps them counter stress caused by social oppression and racism. We also provide an in-depth analysis of what it means to be cool, black, and male in America. Finally, we offer suggestions for intervention, social policy change, and continuing research on cool pose. The voices of Phil and Leroy, black youths who are not unlike many who live in our country's inner cities, are heard throughout.[2]

We hope this book represents a place to begin serious study of cool as an integral aspect of black male masculinity.

What Is Cool Behavior?

Cool is defined by the *American Heritage Dictionary* as "not excited; calm and controlled" and by *A Dictionary of Catch Phrases* as "unafraid, unflustered." *A Dictionary of Slang and Unconventional English* describes cool as a "hippy expression for confidence or self-assuredness." *The Dictionary of American Slang* characterizes cool as being "in complete control of one's emotions; hip but having a quiet, objective, aloof attitude; indifferent to those things considered nonessential to one's individual beliefs, likes, and desires."

By cool pose we mean the presentation of self many black males use to establish their male identity. Cool pose is a ritualized form of masculinity that entails behaviors, scripts, physical posturing, impression management, and carefully crafted performances that deliver a single, critical message: pride, strength, and control. Black males who use cool pose are often chameleon-like in their uncanny ability to change their performance to meet the expectations of a particular situation or audience. They manage the impression they communicate to others through the use of an imposing array of masks, acts, and facades.

For many blacks, life is a relentless performance for the mainstream audience and often for each other. Creating the right image—the most impressive persona—is part of acting in a theater that is seldom dark. Black athletes, with their stylish dunking of the basketball, spontaneous dancing in the end zone, and high-fives handshakes, are cool. The twenty-two-year-old pimp, with his Cadillac and "stable of lace" (prostitutes), is cool. Celebrities such as Miles Davis, Eddie Murphy, and the late Adam Clayton Powell, Jr. are cool. The performance aspect of being cool means that as a black performer leaves his house in the morning, he is "on" and cannot ever completely relax. Even when he is offstage, a black male may feel that he is onstage. And African-American males who are not celebrities find it essential nonetheless to perform.

Glasgow argues that cool is critical to the black male's emerging identity as he develops a distinctive style. This style is highly individualized and is expressed through variations in walk, talk, choice of clothes (threads), and natural or processed hair ("do"). Starting in early adolescence, the young male learns how to develop and maintain his own brand of cool so that he will be "down" instead of "square"; one of the "ins" not one of the "outs." If a young male does not conform to certain subcultural expectations for behavior, he risks not being in. On the streets he learns that being cool is the key to being in—his developing sense of dignity, confidence, and worth depend on it.

In contrast to this emphasis on the expressive side of cool, cool pose may also be a kind of "restrained masculinity": emotionless, stoic, and unflinching. Abrahams views cool as keeping yourself together and remaining well-ordered in the face of disruptive atmospheres. Jones says cool means to be calm and detached, unimpressed by the horrors of daily life.

The Survival Value of Being Cool

Cool pose is a distinctive coping mechanism that serves to counter, at least in part, the dangers that black males encounter on a daily basis. As a performance, cool pose is designed to render the black male visible and to empower him; it eases the worry and pain of blocked opportunities. Being cool is an ego booster for black males comparable to the kind white males more easily find through attending good schools, landing prestigious jobs, and bringing home decent wages.

Cool pose is constructed from attitudes and actions that become firmly entrenched in the black male's psyche as he adopts a facade to ward off the anxiety of second-class status. It provides a mask that suggests competence, high self-esteem, control, and inner strength. It also hides self-doubt, insecurity, and inner turmoil.

By acting calm, emotionless, fearless, aloof, and tough, the African-American male strives to offset an externally imposed "zero" image. Being cool shows both the dominant culture and the black male himself that he is strong and proud. He is somebody. He is a survivor, in spite of the systematic harm done by the legacy of slavery and the realities of racial oppression, in spite of the centuries of hardship and mistrust.

Anomie and Individual Choices for Achieving Success

When a society is in a state of rapid social change, the old rules no longer have sufficient power to inspire conformity. At the same time, new rules that emerge may not receive full commitment from all members of the society. Confusion and anxiety prevail. "Anomie" or "normlessness"—rejection of the rules of the game or confusion over how they apply—opens the door to arbitrary behavior and systematic deviance.

In twentieth century American life, which some observers argue is plagued by anomie, we are surrounded by a culture that places an inordinate value on materialism, success, prestige, personal posses- sions, and wealth. Conspicuous consumption is no longer unusual. Trickery, conning, bank fraud, embezzlement, dishonest advertising and pricing, devious manipulation of corporate structures, insider trading, and tax evasion have become the deviant tools of choice for a middle class bent on the competitive massing of goods and wealth. Violence, toughness, coolness, assault, and theft have become the preferred strategies of the lower-income groups in our society.

Naturally, this leads to a middle- and upper-class stratum of "haves" who fear the lower stratum of "have nots." Residential segregation, the persistence of discrimination in housing and hiring, and the terror of being home alone or walking urban streets at night are all symptoms of anomie in America. Hostility between classes and races—sometimes veiled but often open—contributes to feel- ings of anxiety, suspicion, and despair. For individuals on the lower side of this cultural chasm, the likelihood of personal anxiety, psy- chological disorder, and depression is even greater.

Anomie completes its destruction when those who are shut out of culturally sanctioned means for achieving success become con- vinced, in their anger and frustration, that the rules that govern the mainstream do not apply to them. Merton's theory of individual adaptations and anomie expresses this dilemma well: Socially devi- ant behavior results for certain groups because, while they may share the society's basic goals, they do not share the means for achieving them. Between desire and reality are social, economic, and political barriers that seem impervious to reasonable, everyday effort. Consequently, Merton argues, differential access to the op- portunity structure actually encourages certain individuals to func- tion deviantly in order to obtain rewards of a material or prestigious nature.

Merton identifies individual modes of adaptation that can be used in pursuing societally valued goals: conformity, innovation, re- treatism, ritualism, and rebellion. Success in achieving goals by con- forming to legitimate, conventional means is possible only in the absence of institutionalized barriers, such as racism, or by chance. For the black male, then, conformity is not as effective an adapta- tion as innovation (creating illegitimate or unconventional means to achieve the same goals). Retreatism, in which both the culturally mandated goals and the conventional means are rejected, is also attractive to black males who have given up on the system. Giving up, withdrawing, or refusing to play the game may seem more sensible than continually beating one's head against the wall. Rebellion, in which both goals and means are replaced by new, subcultural goals and means, is also a popular strategy, as indicated by the Black Power Movement. Being tough and substituting a violent life style for more conventional adaptations are also forms of rebellion. Thus, blocked opportunities can result in criminal behavior and antisocial personalities. Cool pose could be defined as a type of innovation in this context.

For the black male, achieving masculinity is complicated by the threats of marginality and anomie that plague his race, and if he is of lower-income status, his social class. The subcultural press toward innovative and rebellious modes of achieving success in the face of remarkable odds shapes his pursuit of masculinity.

Cool—Only One of Many Survival Strategies

Throughout their sojourn in America, black males have developed a myriad of survival techniques necessary to deal with white society. Developing the cool pose is one way that the disenfranchised black male struggles to survive in the face of diminished rights and blemished self-esteem. This survival strategy began under servitude, continued through Reconstruction, legalized discrimination, and ghettoization, and persists today in an era of veiled exclusions and subtler hostilities.

During slavery, the abolitionist movement, slave revolts, the underground railroad, and deliberate acts of defiance or sabotage centered on rebellion and resistance. Uncle Tomism and Samboism, symbolizing the "good Negro" mentality, centered on identification with the oppressor, loyalty, passivity, obedience, docility, accommodation, and submissiveness. Both types of response helped black slave families to survive.

Pettigrew cites several reactions to post-slavery discrimination, from special vigilance to enhanced effort. Some blacks have acquired what Pettigrew calls "an acute protective sensitivity in interracial situations."[3] They develop a sixth sense for detecting cues that spell possible rejection.

Because African-Americans have been forced into the position of out-group existing under the rules of an externally imposed social isolation, they have cultivated their own culture. At the heart of that culture is a subterranean belief that dealings with whites can be risky and deadly. Brutality, dehumanization, shame, and blame can emerge from dealing with American whites. It does not matter that many encounters with whites do not result in pain and inequity. Disenchantment and cynicism go hand in hand with mistrust born of centuries of oppression to generate a reflexive set of coping strategies: "They, and theirs, have been had too many times. A counter-culture, based in large part upon the above impulses, becomes a design, a shield, a complex developmental process, inherent in the lives of Black folk."[4]

Sometimes the coping strategies black males use seem involuntary; always they appear to reflect a narrow range of alternatives "for coping with the immense and overwhelming forces and life situations over which their control was so cruelly limited."[5]

Focus on Cool Pose As a Coping Strategy

Of all the strategies embraced by black males to cope with oppression and marginality, the creation of the cool pose is perhaps the most unique. Presenting to the world an emotionless, fearless, and aloof front counters the low sense of inner control, lack of inner strength, absence of stability, damaged pride, shattered confidence, and fragile social competence that come from living on the edge of society.

For some black males, cool pose represents a fundamental structuring of the psyche—the cool mask belies the rage held in check beneath the surface. For others it is the adoption of a uniquely creative style that serves as a sign of belonging and stature. Black males have learned to use posing and posturing to communicate power, toughness, detachment, and style—self. They have developed a "third eye" that reads interpersonal situations with a special acuity. They have cultivated a keen sense of what to say, and how and when to say it, in order to avoid punishment and pain and to embellish their life chances.

Since their first days as slaves in this land, African-American males have discovered that masking behavior is a supremely useful device. During slavery, black males were masters of cool. Now cool pose has become an integral thread in the fabric of black-black and black-white relationships. It has been exported out of the ghetto into the lives of middle-class black males. Cool has long been blended into jazz and other black music that belongs to all of American society, indeed, the world. And cool has influenced mainstream culture through entertainment, sports, clothing, and the media.

As with most coping strategies, cool pose helps individuals adapt to environmental conditions and neutralize stress. Humans, like other animals, struggle for existence within the context of their social and physical environment. As Darwin pointed out in his theory of evolution, those who survive have found strategies that help them cope with their particular environment. Cool pose is such a strategy for many black males. Wilkinson and Taylor indicate that playing it cool has been a defense for blacks against exploitation. Sometimes being cool may be automatic and unconscious; other times it may be a conscious and deliberate facade. In either case, being cool helps maintain a balance between the black male's inner life and his social environment.

The cool front of black masculinity is crucial for preservation of pride, dignity, and respect. It is also a way for the black male to express bitterness, anger, and distrust toward the dominant society. Cool pose works to keep whites off balance and puzzled about the black man's true feelings.

Being cool enhances the black man's pride and character, helps him cope with conflict and anxiety, and paves an avenue for expressiveness in sports, entertainment, rap-talking, breakdancing, and street cool. It is part of daily life.

Cool pose furnishes the black male with a sense of control, inner strength, balance, stability, confidence, and security. It also reflects these qualities. Cool helps him deal with the closed doors and negative images of himself that he must confront on a daily basis. It may represent one of the richest untapped areas for understanding black male behavior today.

Our book explores the causes, nature, and consequences of cool pose as a dynamic expression of black manhood in America.

Cool is no different between black and white. People killing people for a jacket, because they think it's cool. For a pair of shoes. There's more pressure in the black community to be cool, the negative type of cool. All the commercialism going around. Get what you want.

—Billy, 24

There's another part of cool that everybody in society thinks is having this and having that, but not getting it for yourself, maybe stealing stuff, or whatever. That's a cool person in society, getting stuff that's not even really yours, you're not working for it, you're not having your own job.

—Fran, 21

Look at parents these days; the environment they bring their kids up in is very much polluted. The parents of the olden days used to be people the kids looked up to as example setters. Now, if the father is not anymore in the house, the mother goes and brings another man in, and they fight. This influences the kids. And what do you expect of the kid? He's going to live that violent type of life. He's going to see mommy use that welfare check to buy food, and he says, well, I'm not going to school, I'm going to just live on welfare. I'll just pay my rent and just live on the government. No motive or zeal.

—Dave, 35

I was talking to a girl, she had some money in her hand, ready to pay her rent. She's 14, she should be in school, should be doing something. They blame their parents for what's happened to them, then they just do the same. She's depending on the government every month. There's no advancement in her life. The same cycle. It saddens me that way.

—John, 38

I think youth today, the ones that are doing the drugs and stuff like that, the ones that are so poor, I think that's what could be linked to them— being cool as emotional detachment.

—Gina, 22

Social Stress and Social Symptoms

If black men seem to be losing ground today, it's that they're weary and wounded from trying to thrive in a society that is determined they won't.

—Susan Taylor

While there are whips and men to use them, there will be no peace . . . When men are brothers and men are free, the war will end. Mr. Lincoln Said.

—Earl Robinson[1]

Social Pathology: A Symptom of Oppression

The "war" is not yet over, and African-American males are not yet free. In fact, centuries of racial conflict and oppression in America have placed black males high on the casualty list: Black males have the highest rates (except for native American men) of several important indicators of social stress in the United States.

In every decade since the 1950 census, America's cities have become increasingly non-white, poor, and young, as successive waves of the affluent and middle-aged (mostly whites) flee to the suburbs. Those who are left behind in the ghettos have experienced sharp increases in poverty and uncertainty. As William Julius Wilson points out, "one of the legacies of historic racial and class subjugation in America is a unique and growing concentration of minority residents in the most impoverished areas of large Northeast and Midwest central cities."[2]

Hand in hand with poverty are joblessness, despair, and alienation, the social chemicals that bring the urban crucible to predictable eruptions of violence and a flood of so-called social problems.

The statistics show a clear disadvantage to being born black and male in America: Black males have higher rates than white males on mental disorders, unemployment, poverty, injuries, accidents, infant mortality, morbidity, AIDS, homicide and suicide, drug and alcohol abuse, imprisonment, and criminality; they have poorer incomes, life expectancy, access to health care, and education. We prefer to define these social problems as *social symptoms* of a history of oppression.

Cool pose takes on added significance in light of these symptoms. We suggest that black males have become so conditioned to keeping up their guard against oppression from the dominant society that being cool represents the best safeguard against further mental or physical abuse. We believe that cool pose is both a reaction to stress, and a contributor to stress.

Cool pose is a coping strategy that helps the black male manage his feelings of rage in the face of prejudice and discrimination. But the routine donning of cool pose may also condition the black man to suppress and lose touch with all his feelings, including those that might facilitate nurturant relationships with others. Detachment and numbness are the other side of composure and control, and may contribute to mental disorders and interpersonal difficulties.

Being cool has a profound influence in the lives of black males. It has the potential to help explain why so many black males father children they cannot support or why they engage in such high rates of domestic violence and other types of crime. Cool pose may be involved in stormy intimate male-female relationships, gang behavior, homicide, depression and suicide, adolescent deviance, school failure and disruption, and substance abuse.

Mental Disorders

Mental disorders represent one of the best indicators of stress in the lives of black males; they suffer more often from mental disorders and receive more psychotropic medication and psychiatric hospitalization than black females or the white population.[3] The racial discrepancy is greatest for black males between fifteen and twenty-four years old.

Bulhan writes that since 1922, rates of mental disorders have risen more rapidly for blacks than for whites.[4] Blacks are over-represented in public mental hospitals. The findings on mental disorders and demographic disparity are equally grim. National data on inpatient admissions to state and county mental hospitals show an age-adjusted rate of 509 per 100,000 for black males and 213 per 100,000 for white males. (The rates for black females and white females are 248.5 and 110, respectively.) Admission rates for blacks under forty-four years old are three times those of whites in the same age group. At a time when institutionalization is falling in popularity as a choice for dealing with mental disorder, black males show the slowest rate of decline in that type of mental health care.

The higher prevalence and severity of mental disorders for black males is due partly to problems of diagnosis. Frequently, behavior patterns that mental health professionals perceive as pathological are culturally acceptable, even preferred. Many mental health professionals (and social scientists) lack cultural awareness of black Americans. There is also a scarcity of current, well-researched data on black males, especially regarding cultural variations in definitions of competence and masculinity.

We do not yet know enough about the coping mechanisms some black males use to help counter the stresses they face in this country. In addition to the lack of research in these areas, the phenomenon of cool as a coping mechanism has not been fully explored (as mentioned earlier).

The Disaster of Education

Social, economic, and environmental problems that plague the black community have also contributed to the problems black males may have in school. Dropout rates are high, failure is common, performance below grade level is pervasive, and alienation is epidemic.

Black males are suspended, expelled, pushed out, and take themselves out of school. They leave school for discipline problems twice as often as black females. According to the Children's Defense Fund and White and Parham's *The Psychology of Blacks*, black students are suspended three times more often than whites in elementary school and twice as often in high school. At both levels, black boys have the highest suspension and dropout rates. In some of the nation's largest cities, black male high school dropout rates are astronomical.

Black students are suspended for longer periods and more frequently compared to white students in both elementary and secondary schools. In 1981, almost half of all seventeen-year-old black males were woefully behind their appropriate grade level or had dropped out of school altogether.

A Department of Education survey showed that in 1989 17.5 percent of black males (aged eighteen and nineteen) had left high school without graduating, compared to 14.4 percent of white males. Naturally, dropping out has an enormous impact on functional illiteracy and, ultimately, marketable job skills, employment, and the ability to seek out legitimate means of proving manhood. Kozol estimates that rates of functional illiteracy for black males hover around an astonishing 45 percent. Since 1976, the percentage of black high school graduates, especially males, who enroll in higher education has steadily declined.

Conflicts between black males and (often white) school personnel suggest that young black men are frequently pushouts rather than dropouts. While many black males are suspended from school for fighting, just as many are suspended for culture-specific behaviors— strutting, rapping, woofing, playing the dozens, using slang, wearing hats or expressive clothes, or wearing pants with loosened belts. In other words, African-American students are sometimes suspended for behavior they consider to be stylish or cool.

In *Ribbin', Jivin' and Playin' the Dozens*, Foster hypothesizes that teachers suspend black males for certain cool behaviors and attitudes because they perceive them as negative, rude, arrogant, intimidating, sexually provocative, and threatening—and therefore not conducive to learning. Black males are more likely than whites to be recommended for special education, classes for the emotionally disturbed, and remedial classes; they are also more likely to be physically punished and labeled as mildly mentally handicapped. These recommendations may be justified in some cases but—given the lack of cultural sensitivity of white teachers, counselors, and school administrators—they are yet another form of subtle racism with devastating consequences for black youths. Schools revolve around middle-class norms and expectations. Most teachers are white, and many lack the cultural insight, training, and sensitivity to recognize that young black males may perceive expressive and cool behavior as a source of pride and do not necessarily define such behavior as negative or disruptive.

The lower achievement scores of black males are symptomatic of the legacy of centuries of educational discrimination against blacks. That legacy will not be removed overnight.

Unemployment

The effect of stress on the mental health of black males is further complicated by high unemployment. In *The State of Black America*, the Urban League reports that since 1960, unemployment rates for blacks have been double those for whites.[5] Further, the Census Bureau report, *America's Black Population: 1970–1982*, shows that joblessness among blacks increased 140 percent between 1972 and 1982. Not surprisingly, the Bureau of Labor Statistics reports an unemployment rate of 11.8 percent for black males in 1990 compared to 4.8 percent for white males. By 1982, black unemployment was the highest ever recorded in post-World War II history; black unemployment reached 18.9 percent as compared to 8.6 percent for whites.[6] But the statistics for black teenage joblessness, especially for males, are even more alarming. In 1987, the unemployment rate among black youths was 34 percent—twice the rate of 17 percent for teens of all races combined.[7] Black unemployment remains at record high levels as we enter the 1990s.

The Sting of Poverty

Swinton elaborates on the effect of federal government cuts on black poverty. Although black poverty dropped slightly in 1984, the rate of 34 percent was still higher than it had been in any of the ten years preceding the Reagan Administration. That Administration's so-called recovery hardly made a dent in the average black male's chances of finding work. The 1990 rate was 31.9 percent.

As a result of poverty, black median income has held steady or dropped. The gap between black and white incomes has actually widened. Single parent families suffer the most. In 1990, the median income for a black family maintained by a woman was $12,100 compared to $19,500 for white-female-headed families. The median income of black couple families was about $33,800 compared to over $40,000 for whites. The median income of all black families was $21,400 compared to the white family's $36,900.

Children Too Soon, Too Fast

Even in the face of crushing poverty, most black males have accepted the basic masculine goals of wanting to raise and provide for a family. The inclination to take this road to manhood is strong, despite obstacles to supporting families; children are an important statement for declaring manhood. One way black males make that statement is through sexual promiscuity and procreation.

It is much more difficult for the black man to enact the traditional male role successfully than it is for the black woman to establish a positive female role. She is more likely to complete school and to have the opportunity to work—she can also have a child and care for it. *Tally's Corner*, Liebow's study of black men in Washington, D. C., suggests that the black man who experiences economic role failure may compensate by defining masculinity in terms of being able to impregnate women and produce children (especially sons) who are extensions of himself. Or he can define manhood in terms of multiple relationships and sexual partners. For some black males there is an inseparable link between self-esteem and the ability to have affairs with women who produce their children. This is one way they can be productive, creative, and feel that they are making a tangible contribution to family and community.

Difficulty supporting a baby and its mother was a fact of slavery and is still a problem today. Perhaps it is the survival instinct that keeps black couples from letting a lack of funds deter them from mating. If poverty prevailed, America's racially based social class system would have spelled near extinction for poor blacks by now. For the lower-income black male, the joys of fatherhood lie in the act of procreation and in knowing that he has progeny, not necessarily in knowing that he can support his babies. However, recent work indicates that most black males who have the opportunity to work do in fact support their children.

African-American males may consciously and unconsciously reinforce with their brothers the idea that sexual promiscuity and procreation are cool because they symbolize manhood. They also afford entertainment, recreation, stimulation, and the pleasures of female companionship and adulation.

Unfortunately, promiscuity contributes to teenage pregnancy rates that are twice as high among blacks as among whites (163 per 1,000 versus 83 per 1,000, respectively). In 1980, nearly one out of every ten black teenage females gave birth (9.5 percent) as opposed to only one of every twenty-five white females (4.5 percent).[8] Predictably, over half (58 percent) of the black children in this country are born outside of marriage.[9]

The consequences of early pregnancy and promiscuity can be devastating for black females, causing male-female conflict and various forms of abuse. Straus and his colleagues have found that wife abuse is almost four times as common among black families as compared to white families. Black husbands are three times more likely than white husbands to hit their wives or engage in domestic violence.

In addition, promiscuity contributes to other problems in the black community. The spread of venereal disease and AIDS, a direct result of promiscuity, has taken its toll on the black community. The Centers for Disease Control reports that AIDS hits black males over two and one-half times more often than white males. Blacks represent 25 percent of all reported AIDS cases, while black males account for 23 percent of all male cases, according to Gibbs.

Sexual promiscuity also affects the divorce rate. According to the Census Bureau, the black divorce rate in 1982 was 220 per 1,000 marriages versus 107 per 1,000 white marriages. Oliver indicates that black male-female conflict leads to assault and murder of black females at a greater rate than do the intimate relationships of any other racial or ethnic group in the United States. Male-female conflict may develop when a female criticizes her partner for his inability to support the family. Or when she raises her voice (even worse if it is "around the guys"). He takes this as further insult to an already jeopardized sense of manhood and self-esteem, and may become violent to save face. Many black men feel that, even though they may not be able to control how society treats them, at the very least they should be able to control "their women."

According to Hampton, sexual infidelity, emotional and physical abuse, anger, revenge, jealousy, and self-defense inspire black females to murder their black male partners at comparatively high rates. At Renz Correctional Facility in Missouri, almost a quarter of the women serving thirty to fifty-year sentences are there for killing abusive mates.

Blacks, Masculinity, and the Military

Being locked out of the mainstream may contribute to the comparatively high number of black males who volunteer for military service. Lack of education and jobs pushes black men and women toward the armed services for training, income, and a modicum of security. If access to mainstream opportunities were color blind, blacks would comprise exactly 13 percent of the military—their proportion in the general population in the United States. Instead, they account for 21 percent of all branches of the military. During the Gulf War, blacks made up 20 percent of the deployment; one half of all the women serving in the Gulf were black.[10]

Adherence to masculine toughness also channels many black males into active duty. The need to prove their manhood, Staples argues, has contributed to their disproportionate involvement in such comparatively dangerous military units as paratroopers and special forces. Not only do black males volunteer to serve in special units at a higher rate than white males, but there is some evidence that institutionalized racism may deliver them to front-line duty, death, and suffering at higher rates.

Unfortunately, as the Gulf War and other wars have proved, the military is not only a route out of the ghetto, but it is also about killing and dying. Many black men die or are wounded proving their masculinity and trying to feel powerful while serving in these special military units. For example, in the Vietnam War, a quarter of all deaths were black males. We must ask if this pattern would remain true if blacks had equal access to opportunity, economic success, and other avenues for validation of manhood.

Babies and Men Who Die Too Soon

Infant Mortality and Life Expectancy

Especially in conditions of poverty and poor prenatal health care, children having children are at personal risk and are more likely to produce babies with low birth weight and illness during childhood. As Gibbs points out, infant mortality rates are highest among babies born to teen mothers, and the rates are twice as high among blacks compared to whites.

The outlook for those who survive to adulthood is equally bleak: Black males have the lowest life expectancy of any group in the United States, except for native Americans. In fact, black males in Harlem have a shorter life expectancy than men in the third-world country of Bangladesh; except for people over age eighty-five, black males are dying at a higher rate than any other group at any age.[11] With the high probability of stress from threatening economic and social conditions, it is not surprising that the black male's life expectancy of sixty-five years is the lowest of any sex or racial group. This compares with seventy-four years for black women, seventy-two years for white men, and seventy-nine years for white women.

Moreover, such self-destructive and high-risk behaviors as drive-by shootings, the use and availability of guns, gang violence, and confrontational behaviors that test limits with parents, teachers, and police can also lead to punishment, harm, and high injury rates.

In *Young, Black, and Male in America: An Endangered Species*, Gibbs uses the term "the new morbidity" to describe how young black males are overrepresented in deaths caused by homicide, accident, and suicide. Gibbs argues that drug and alcohol abuse plays a major role in most of these deaths: Combined, they account for over 75 percent of deaths among young men between fifteen and twenty-four years old.

Gibbs feels that most of the deaths are caused by social rather than biological factors, products of high-risk activities, self-destructive behaviors, and deviant life-styles. We agree and we believe that cool pose may be a key element that interconnects risk and death: Self-destructive, risk-taking behavior serves for some black males as a way to convince others of their masculinity. Drugs, alcohol, and guns are props used in a cool performance that may lead to death, rather than to validation as a male.

Homicide

Because many black males employ cool pose without regard for appropriateness of time and place, acting cool can cause severe problems. Some black males will not allow themselves to express any form of weakness, such as fear or backing off from a fight, even if retreating would prevent violence or arrest.

When cool behaviors are placed ahead of acknowledging and

dealing with true fears or needs, pent-up emotions and frustrations result, which are then released in aggressive behavior toward those who are closest to the black male—other black people. Hence, cool pose may contribute to one of the more complex problems in the black community today: black-on-black crime.

There is a one in twenty-one chance that a young black male will be murdered by the time he reaches his twenty-fifth birthday. In 1977, more black males died as a result of homicide than perished in the Vietnam War from 1963 to 1972. Even though black males and females were overrepresented in the forces sent to the Middle East during the Gulf War, black males are still at greater risk on the streets of this nation's cities.

Rose and McClain, in their recent book on black homicide in America, argue that the environment of large urban communities increases the likelihood of black male victimization by murder. Murder is the major cause of the higher death rate among black males, especially those between twenty-five and forty-four years old. And, according to the Centers for Disease Control, homicide is the leading cause of death for black males aged fifteen to twenty-four. The overall rate of homicide for blacks is five and one-half times higher than that of whites.[12] In 1985 alone, over 1,900 young black males were murdered. Furthermore, over 90 percent of them were murdered by other black males, most of them, like their victims, under twenty-four years of age.

Over 54 percent of the black population is under twenty-four, compared to only 42 percent of whites.[13] With such a large proportion of black males in this age bracket, the impact of their violent behavior will be amplified if nothing is done to change the prevailing trends. Firearms are the weapon of choice in homicide cases. Most national and local studies have found that the majority of black victims are relatives, friends, or acquaintances of the offenders. Reasons for homicide range from street holdups to drug trades to sexual jealousy to gang fights.[14]

The homicide rate is increasing by distressing leaps among black males, especially young urban blacks. Washington, D.C., for example, which is a city heavily populated by African-Americans, has become known as the nation's murder capital; most of the victims and perpetrators are young black males. In 1990, over 400 murders were committed. One black person dies per day, on the average, a trend that continues into 1991. Most of them are young males.

Accidents and Self-Destructive Behaviors

The second leading cause of death among young black males is accidents—almost 2,000 black youths die or are severely disabled by accidents and injuries each year.[15] Accidents not only contribute to the high mortality rate of black males, but reflect the self-destructive, risk-taking life-styles of many. Motor vehicle fatalities represent the highest percentage of deaths and injuries caused by accidents. Many single-car fatalities are the result of aggressive, high-risk driving, such as "leaning-in-the-car," one-arm driving, and drag racing. For males who drag race in cities, the likelihood of accident is greatly increased because of poor street conditions.

The suicide rate among black males has skyrocketed in recent years and is now "the third leading cause of death among black males in the 18 to 29 year-old age group."[16] Toughness and masculinity may also deter black males from visiting doctors or following prescribed treatment until serious illness or disability results. In addition, self-destruction is expressed in such habits as smoking and substance abuse.

Death by Stress

Of course, poverty has a powerful effect on the health status, life expectancy, and mortality rates of blacks. In 1982, the U. S. Department of Health and Human Services conducted a study of the fifteen leading causes of death and concluded that a disproportionate number of black men were losing their lives to stress-related diseases.[17] In another Health and Human Services report, *The Secretary's Task Force on Black and Minority Health*, Heckler elaborates further: "Blacks reported lower rates of disabling heart disease than whites at each level. However, because the rates decrease as income rises and there are proportionately more blacks among the lower income strata, the overall black rates of disabling heart disease are higher."[18] Similar correlations can be found between education and other diseases. Obviously, lack of income and education must be recognized as risk factors for disease and death in blacks.

Cancer and cerebrovascular disease also are leading causes of death among young black males and are complicated by high stress jobs, poor nutrition, and substance abuse. Black males die at a higher rate than white males from such causes as hypertension, cirrhosis of the liver, heart disease, tuberculosis, diabetes, and lung diseases.

Escaping with Alcohol and Drugs

Black males often use alcohol or drugs to help ease the stress and agitations of their daily lives. They also engage in substance use and abuse to be cool—part of the "scene." All too often, black males, like other substance users, become hopelessly addicted with little chance of working out of the addiction trap. Although there is some disagreement, it seems that rates of heavy drinking and alcoholism are significantly higher among blacks than they are among whites.[19]

Although white males drink earlier, by middle age black males consume more alcohol than white males, and a higher percentage of black males are diagnosed with alcohol-related disorders. Consequently, problem drinking is more common among blacks than it is among whites, which suggests a close relationship between stress and destructive behavior. The consumption of alcohol and drugs in black communities can be viewed as an attempt to cope with social and psychological frustrations resulting from unemployment and underemployment, poverty and inflation, inadequate housing, family problems, and discrimination.

The impact of substance abuse is amplified by its role in premature and low-birth-weight babies, illnesses, premature deaths, inability to hold employment, accidents, rape, and other forms of violence. As a result, more black males are incarcerated than any other group in this country.

Criminality and Incarceration

The prevalence of violence among black males is reflected in data on arrest and criminality. African-Americans comprise 13 percent of the population but are disproportionately represented among both perpetrators and victims of violent crime. Black men are more likely to be arrested, convicted, and incarcerated than white males (even for the same behavior) and have the highest rate of incarceration of all race-gender groups.[20]

Arrest data compiled by the FBI for 1983 reveal that blacks represented 27.3 percent of all persons arrested. In 1984, a U.S. Department of Justice study found that blacks accounted for 47.5 percent of the arrests for violent crimes. Furthermore, the Uniform Crime Report shows that blacks comprised 35.7 percent of all arrests for index crimes: criminal homicide, forcible rape, robbery, aggravated assault, burglary, breaking and entering, larceny, theft, motor vehicle theft, and arson. In addition, in 1983 blacks accounted for 49.6 percent of the individuals who were arrested for murder and nonnegligent manslaughter.[21]

The situation is worsening. In 1988, blacks constituted 53 percent of all individuals arrested for murder, 41 percent of those arrested for aggravated assault, and 36 percent of those arrested for simple assault. Incarceration rates also confirm the high violence trends among blacks. According to Oliver, in 1986 black males represented over 47 percent of the prison population in the United States. Between 1978 and 1982, black males were eight times more likely to be in prison than were white males.[22] There may be at least a partial explanation for the high rate of incarceration among black males: low income and higher arrest and conviction rates than whites. In 1975, the Census Bureau reported that almost 60 percent of young black prison inmates entered with incomes of less than $3,000 annually.

The linkages among race, poverty, and crime are obvious. While prisoners are likely to be guilty of some legally defined crimes, the overwhelming convergence of negative indicators around black males suggests the operation of more insidious institutional acts of violence against them (both symbolic and real) for which there are no legal definitions, prohibitions, or remedies. That is, underlying structural violence that jeopardizes the equal opportunity of blacks to achieve life, liberty, and happiness in an allegedly free society breeds violence in its enraged victim. This is not a new idea; black men, however, pay for its neglect with a high price in isolation and alienation.

The current social climate—including the move toward conservatization of the United States Supreme Court—calls for harsher retribution against criminals at the same time that it demands cuts in programs to counter the equally criminal social and economic forces that grease the slide to crime. Homelessness and desperately crowded prisons are shrill reminders that our system has failed terribly, especially for black males.

The Interplay of Destructive Forces

Poverty, unemployment, educational problems, alcohol and drug abuse, homicide, suicide, incarceration, poor health, low life expectancy, and high mortality are intricately interrelated. And they are all related to the web of racism and oppression.

White racism and discrimination have long created a crisis in character for whites and a crisis in survival for blacks. In *The Black Male in America*, Taylor notes that racism, as a central feature of American social life, creates systematic stigmatization of blacks more than any other minority group. Aggression and dogmatic beliefs ultimately debase black men: Their self-image is discredited. Even a black male who is unknown to whites will be seen first as black and second as a person. This stereotypical albatross is worn by all blacks, but because of fear during slavery and Reconstruction of black men taking white women, black males wear it every moment of their lives.

Black males, in addition to being affected by individual and group racism, are also affected by institutionalized racism, which in fact can have longer-term and more damaging effects.[23] Institutionalized racism refers to the policies and rules, traditional practices, and informal networks that operate in major social institutions (politics, economics, and education) to keep minorities "in their place" and out of the mainstream.

For example, in *Racism: A Philosophic Probe*, Okolo argues that residential ghettoization of blacks away from dominant white American society is a blatant reflection of racism created, maintained, and condoned by white institutions (in this case, banks, mortgage companies, real estate agents, and insurance companies). Some observers might argue that in recent years some blacks have chosen to live in predominantly black neighborhoods as an expression of solidarity and ethnic identity. Voluntary segregation is not ghettoization. Historically, however, blacks have had no choice as to where they could live in relation to whites. Inner-city ghettos were, and are, a symptom of a deeply divided society.

Sadly, even when institutions change their racist and exclusionary practices, the message may be slow to filter down to the young black man living in poverty. Mancini, in *Strategic Styles*, tells of a black teenager who is looking for a job in Roxbury. He tells his father that he plans to inquire at a local shoe manufacturer. His father, who many years earlier was turned away by the same company—because he was black—warns his son not to bother. The youth avoids the company and never discovers that, in fact, it has hired blacks from the neighborhood for years.

Cuts in Government Programs

Black unemployment and institutionalized racism have been further compounded by government cuts in federally sponsored programs. The Urban League reports that government cuts in the early 1980s slashed programs that serve children and young adults, including job training. Cuts in mental health services, Aid to Families with Dependent Children, and programs to prevent child abuse have further placed the black child in jeopardy before he even reaches the teen years, when the search for employment begins.

During the Reagan years, reductions in federal money earmarked for cities (through the Community Development Act and other programs) translated into tangible losses in employment training, housing and community development, health care, and social services. Programs targeted toward the unemployed and families with young children were especially hard hit.

This trend continues into the 1990s, as the so-called peace dividend is drained into military spending and the savings and loan bailout. Federal cuts have had a measurable impact on the poor. For example, devastating slashes in one of the nation's most successful federal programs, Women, Infants and Children (WIC), have taken thousands of poor children away from their only opportunity to receive nutrition monitoring and food assistance.

Social stress, then, is the product of a powerful concatenation of historical patterns and current policies. The greater participation of black males in pathological behaviors can be viewed only in this context. Strong adults emerge from strong children. The nation is apparently not yet prepared to ensure that black males are supported in their efforts to become strong men or that all children have the best chance for success. It is within this intricate matrix of barriers and blockades to maximum individual achievement that we place the genesis of cool pose as a coping strategy among young African-American males.

Being cool is both style and materialism. Younger people place emphasis on what kind of car you have, the clothes you wear. But they also place it on how you act. If you have the clothes, but you don't act quite right, you won't get the same respect. It's a combination of both of them. But if you're just cool, but you don't have anything, they don't respect you either. I would like a guy that's cool for himself, not because he's got a nice car, or whatever. Where'd he get that car from, you know?

—Fran, 21

Being cool is like having a character. It varies from person to person how he walks, how he talks, how he presents himself to society. There's no specific walk.

—Jackson, 19

It's like this: if somebody picks on you or something, and you don't fight back, they'll call you a chicken. But the opposite of that, if you fight back, get them on the fence or something, you're cool.

—Donny, 17

You don't even have to fight, like combat. You can be cool for other reasons. It's almost like a respect, how you should get along. People say, he's cool, like in other words, don't bother with him. You can be respected for your dressing. It doesn't always have to be physical, although that plays a big part in it. People will respect you because you can defend yourself.

—Donny, 17

Most people walk with their head up. Pretty confident about what they're doing and where they're going and that's what makes us look at them in that light of being cool.

—Joe, 20

Cool is keeping cool, the guy who's calm, level-headed in all situations.

—Jackson, 19

3

Cool Pose and Masculinity

See, you don't let things bother you too much. Start letting things bother you, you're going to lose your cool.

— *Phil*

When you're a man, it makes you think you're a strong star out there. It makes you feel like you're a man. Then I can deal . . . I can do anything I want to do.

— *Phil*

Playing It Cool

The black male is socialized to view every white man as a potential enemy, every symbol of the dominant system as a potential threat. As a result, he is reluctant to expose his innermost feelings. Playing it cool becomes the mask of choice. Cool pose is a well-developed and creative art; it also exacts a stiff price in repressed feelings and suppressed energy.

Since the days of slavery, African-Americans have used coolness to express themselves without risking punishment. Playing it cool becomes a routinized, stylized method for expressing the aggressive masculinity that pervades black life. Grier and Cobbs describe a black man, overwhelmed with conflict, whose feelings threaten to erupt. Rather than reveal his true feelings, he presents a serene exterior in a brave attempt to project a composed, controlled self-image. He may fear that the revelation of deep feelings of hatred, anger, or inner turmoil will unleash aggression against the white world, thereby inviting punishment. Although whites hold their feelings in on occasion (and for many of the same reasons), the price paid by the black male for letting his emotions slip out into the fabric of daily life is much higher. For him, it is far more important to maintain the cool exterior, the facade, the lie.

Perkins believes that being cool is a trademark of sophistication that proves that the black male can function well under pressure. Coolness is a stabilizer that minimizes threatening situations and earns respect from others. Cool pose may be linked with slickness, neat appearance, verbal manipulation, and the ability to stay out of trouble. Although the "cool cat" may appear indifferent to the problems around him or seem impervious to pain, frustration, or death, he is unlikely to allow his deeper feelings to surface. If he lifts his protective shield, he risks appearing timid. Cool pose helps him achieve a stern, impersonal masculinity in the face of adversity.

Perhaps cool pose can be understood best as impression management or performance, along the lines of Erving Goffman's dramaturgical analysis. Cool pose is a carefully crafted persona based on power and control over what the black male says and does—how he "plays" his role. For the black male who has limited control or access to conventional power or resources, cool pose is empowering. He can appear on the stage of life as competent, in control, playing to a diversity of audiences with flair and uniqueness. The act is not so much from dishonest, cunning, or manipulative motives as it is essential for continued survival.

The performance must, of course, be credible. Theatricality must always be appropriate for the stage and props at hand. The meaning of the performance is negotiated with each new audience and with others in the interaction.

A One-Dimensional Image of Maleness

The ironclad facade of cool pose is a signature of true masculinity, but it is one-dimensional. If it fails, masculinity fails. Coolness and manhood are so intricately intertwined that letting the cool mask fall, even briefly, feels threatening. This is the facade that provides security in an insecure world. This is the mask that provides outer calm in the midst of inner turmoil. Because staying cool is so critical to the core of masculine identity for many black males, it is worth an enormous investment of physical and psychological energy—every day.

For those whose masculinity is defined so uniquely by the cool pose, unmasking is equivalent to being stripped of identity and being defenseless in a hostile environment. As Vontress points out, the black male is reluctant to expose his real self to anyone, even to his close friends or spouse. Exposing himself could mean loss of autonomy and being engulfed or destroyed by a society that he perceives as racist.

Cool As the Ultimate Control

For many black males cool pose is a way to say, "you might break my back but not my spirit." Cool pose is the black man's last-ditch effort for masculine self-control. Folb elaborates on the importance of control to black males: Power over one's self is the most important form of power, "particularly in an environment where manipulation and control over others have been raised to the level of a fine art, where contest and game playing are often the rule, not the exception."[1]

The young black male sees control in terms of having a weak or a strong mind. If he loses control, he becomes dangerously vulnerable to pressures that he fears will undermine him or "blow his mind." Cool helps him get and stay in control over his psychological and social space.

The Tough Side of Cool

Beyond masking, to be cool may mean to "keep up your dukes"—to be tough. Some black males structure their behavior to give the impression that they are independent, always in control, and emotionally detached. Tough talk and aggressive posturing are valid ways of expressing coolness.

Cool pose can be used as a facade to advertise the black male's willingness to resort to violence to resolve interpersonal conflict. Oliver says that adherence to the toughness norm is displayed through symbolic gestures that communicate cool in the face of threats to the black male's self-image or physical safety. It can also be used to veil concern or guilt when he is involved in violence. Symbolic displays of toughness defend his identity and gain him respect; they can also promote camaraderie and solidarity among black males.

The black male's cultural signature is his cool. It is sometimes the only source of pride, dignity, and worth in the absence of the outward status symbols of materialism and title that mark success in American culture. His status rides on his ability to communicate, through human encounters, the most important information about himself: his coolness. Because it is so prized, preserving cool becomes an end in itself. Glasgow contends that the cool urban youth would rather go down in defeat or retreat than "blow his cool." He relates this story:

> A brother was hemmed in by twenty five cops and the dude didn't have nothing with him, and knew that them mother fuckers was going to head whip him. Man, that brother didn't move back an inch. He just put up his dukes and went at them cops with their carbines and shotguns and riot sticks. Man, they beat the shit out of him, man messed him all up—but that brother was cool.[2]

This is a story of toughness and survival. Being cool obviously means being in control and invulnerable in the face of crushing odds. It means weaving a web of insensitivity to pain and trouble that cannot be cut through by knives, clubs, guns, or words.

The tough side of cool is that it involves risk-taking. To remain cool against well-armed police is to risk injury, imprisonment, or death. Lyman and Scott describe coolness as poise under pressure. The cool male can act and talk in a smoothly controlled fashion even in the tightest of corners. He can remain detached even in the face of emotionally charged situations. Playing it cool is a survival technique par excellence and a risky business.

Masculine Attainment

Masculine attainment refers to the persistent quest for gender identity among all American males. Being a male means to be responsible and a good provider for self and family. For black males, this is not a straightforward achievement. Outlets for achieving masculine pride and identity, especially in political, economic, and educational systems, are more fully available to white males than to black males. This in turn restricts the black man's ability to achieve in family systems, to take care of a wife and family, or to be a present and supportive father.

Cazenave asks a telling question: "What happens to black men who accept society's notions of what it takes to be a man but are denied the resources to 'earn' their masculinity through traditional channels?"[3] He argues, and we agree, that recognition of this "precarious predicament" is a key to understanding black masculinity.

The black male's path toward manhood is lined with pitfalls of racism and discrimination, negative self-image, guilt, shame, and fear. He struggles toward manhood with a sense that he lacks something; he is *manqué*. His schools place him in lower achievement groups; teachers speak of language deficits; economists call him disadvantaged; and psychologists refer to him as disordered. Keil believes that, "Having been denied a natural development of his sense of manliness, he must constantly prove to himself that he is a man."[4] This "masculine protest" can become the constant thread woven throughout the black male's daily interaction: "I am worthy, I am powerful, I am a man."

The humiliating double bind of having to prove manhood while being denied access to the legitimate tools with which to do so creates emotional drudgery for black males. This double bind has been recognized by many observers of the black male's situation in America. Like other men, black males want to be productive and responsible citizens—but can they? Do they have real choices? Sitting on the margins of American society makes those choices distressingly narrow.

This dilemma was noted as early as 1940 by E. Franklin Frazier. He believed that black men did not fail to provide for their families because they did not want to; they failed because they could not do so. In fact, Frazier found that black males had thoroughly internalized the traditional norms of American patriarchy. When they were able to conform to these norms, they did so gladly and even overconformed in some cases. After emancipation, many black men still did not find the steady, remunerative work necessary to provide for their families. Many fled to the urban north to seek stable work, only to find a more subtle form of discrimination where they hoped they would find none. Underemployment, seasonal and inconsistent employment, low pay, and being the last hired and first fired plagued their attempts to provide with reliability. These same economic woes persist today.

Rainwater underscores the marginality of blacks that deprives them of acquiring the skills and resources necessary to accomplish legitimate social goals. Acceptance of the traditional male as responsible provider also persists. Cazenave, in a study of fifty-four employed black letter carriers, asked: "What do you think it means to be a man today?" Forty-one percent of the responses centered on one word: responsibility. Other prominent responses included hard work, ambition, and firm guiding principles. These men defined masculinity as a "complex, demanding, and changing role."[5] They zeroed in on the masculine role of provider. They knew that income and job security were keys in being able to provide for their families. Being a man was equated with taking care of one's family. They clearly understood this norm, and those who had the resources to execute it felt proud.

Billingsley writes that the wider society does not generally appreciate the fact that many poor blacks live in nuclear families headed by hard-working men who, nonetheless, find their paychecks embarassingly inadequate to lift them out of poverty. Hill and Ackiss support the more positive model of the lower-class father in the family context in their study of the all-black community of Boley, Oklahoma. They allude to the stability of husbands/fathers and to families in general who are oriented to conventional middle-class values and mores.

In a study of husband/father roles in a predominantly low-income neighborhood in a southern city, Robinson, Bailey, and Smith found that most of the literature on black fathers portrays them as failing to give their children an appropriate image of a father. Yet, the researchers also discovered that these men serve as positive models and play major roles in providing for their families. They act as disciplinarian, play with their children, and make family decisions. And when questioned about it, these men clearly perceive their role as that of main provider for the family.

Cazenave studied the impact of racism, socioeconomic status, and age on the sex-role perceptions of black men versus white men of similar socioeconomic status and age. He found the black male to be more traditional in the way he embraces typical masculine values: aggressiveness, being competitive, being successful at work, protecting his family, and self-confidence. But he is also more likely than the white male to place a heavy emphasis on warmth, gentleness, and standing up for his beliefs.

Violence and Masculinity

Why do black males often emphasize masculine values that result in violence and other forms of destructive behavior? For black males, two of the most common responses to blocked opportunities are rigidity and aggression. In American society, a potpourri of violence, toughness, and symbolic control over others constitutes a prime means through which black men can demonstrate masculinity.[6]

As we have seen, American society has not provided many black males with legitimate channels or resources for developing a strong sense of masculinity, status, and respect. Violence has become a readily available and seemingly realistic tool for achieving these critical social rewards; it is in this sense that violence can even become a form of achievement when everything else has failed. Sociologists refer to this as the resource theory of violence; that is, violence is viewed as a resource that can be used to achieve desired goals and status when other routes to achievement are blocked.

If he lacks the resources to maintain his position as symbolic head of his family, the black male may seek to maintain a semblance of position through other means, including the use of superior physical force. The language of violence is one way to write a more dominative masculine script.

Many black males have attempted to assert themselves by adopting a defiant, confrontational style known in black folklore as the "bad nigga" or "badman" who "refuses to accept the subservient position allocated to blacks."[7] Badmen, such as John Henry Stagalee [Railroad Bill], Shine, or boxer Jack Johnson, had one thing in common: they used a conscious show of some type of physical force to prove themselves.

Folb links masculine protest to violence:

> There is a need to prove oneself, to demonstrate an ability to "dish it out" and to "take it"—even in the face of overwhelming odds. . . . A great pride is taken in being tough. The more potential danger inherent in the situation, the greater the proving ground for one's "bad-assed" ability.[8]

Toughness, violence, and disregard of death and danger become the hallmark of survival in a world that does not respond to reasonable efforts to belong and achieve. The frustration that inevitably wells up from believing in a role that one cannot fulfill effectively spills over into other ways of proving masculinity: being cool, being tough, and sinking deeper and deeper into the masking behaviors that remove the sting of failure.

Coolness and Compulsive Masculinity

American society also prescribes and reinforces a male image that centers on being tough, emotionally unexpressive, detached, and self-reliant. The image of the Marlboro man slips off the billboard into the male psyche. Black men buy into this image as readily as white men but are not as likely to have the resources to bring the image into reality.

Cool pose gives the black male his greatest sense of pride and masculinity. The risk-taking and self-destructive aspects of cool pose are often symbolically expressed as part of a compulsive masculinity—what some have called *macho* and what Oliver has called the "compulsive masculine alternative." In compulsive masculinity, typical masculine values become a rigid prescription for toughness, sexual promiscuity, manipulation, thrill-seeking, and a willingness to use violence to resolve interpersonal conflict. These values, perpetuated through male-to-male transmission in a tightly knit street culture, lead toward smoking, drug and alcohol abuse, fighting, sexual conquest, dominance, and crime.

Compulsive masculinity is an alternative to traditional definitions of manhood, compensating for feelings of shame, powerlessness, and frustration. Being a man becomes redefined in terms that lead to destruction of self and others. Staying cool ensures that the destructiveness remains palatable.

Proving his masculinity is a daily chore for the black male. It can never be taken for granted. How does he cope with the quest for manhood?

A cool guy is a respectful person toward himself and toward others. And that goes for relations with members of his sex and the opposite sex. It depends on the intensity of that coolness. Sometimes men can treat women disrespectful, treat their friends better than their women. With their friends, they're all the same, and they know how they're supposed to be in their neighborhood. With their woman, that person is testing their cool.

—Gina, 22

There is emphasis on cool. The youth today, you just walk out on any corner and you can see it. People will say, wow, we gotta go ride, or look at his chain. That's what the emphasis is on. The younger generation is more materialistic, because you have to be in with the crowd and if you're not in with the crowd, you're all by yourself.

—Dorothy, 40

A group who see themselves as being cool guys, having a cool character, they're overbound with their definition of cool . . . they see themselves as being "bad" ("supercool"). They exceed the limits of being cool. They feel that whenever there is something that's there, and they want to get it, they've got to get it. If they don't, they've got to get it by some illegal means.

—Billy, 24

In Search of Pride and Manhood

> We real cool. We
> Left school. We
> Lurk late. We
> Strike straight. We
> Sing sin. We
> Thin gin. We
> Jazz June. We
> Die soon.
>
> —Gwendolyn Brooks

> You're going to find that when you start getting out there dealin' with whites, that you're going to have to use a type of cool somewhere.
>
> —Phil

The Positive Side of Being Cool

Cool pose is an important strategy that some black males have developed for dealing creatively with the realities of everyday life. But it is a paradoxical style: The elements that bring the black male peace of mind and control are the same elements that ultimately cause him problems.

Cool pose is capable of producing both negative and positive consequences. It contributes to a masculinity that includes dynamic and positive qualities: dignity, respect, control, self-esteem, and social competence. It helps protect the African-American male's self-image and enables him to cope with assaults on his manhood. Ironically, cool pose can also inject strain into his most intimate relationships, get him in trouble with authorities, and reinforce an aloofness that stems from living too far from his deeper emotions.

In this chapter, we elaborate on the positive aspects of being cool and explore the question of how cool can backfire to complicate the problems black males already face in modern America.

Being Cool As a Form of Social Competence

The contribution of cool pose as an effective expression of social competence deserves special attention. Cool pose helps provide the black male with a type of social competence—the ability to deal effectively with his environment. For black males, the environment is often harsh, cold, and mined with the stumbling blocks of racism and social oppression. Social competence requires a mustering of his best intellectual, physical, and emotional skills. Cool pose is one weapon in the armament of social competence. It is directly linked to what Washington highlights as two key elements in the black man's ability to surmount his daily struggles: coping and mastery.

Washington maintains that in order to be socially competent, the black man must be able to accurately read his place in the social structure. He must be able to clearly see where he stands. And he must also understand which behaviors are appropriate to his place. We would add that the black male must be able to figure out which behaviors are going to place him at risk, even though he may choose to engage in them in order to break out of his place and achieve higher levels of social competence.

Historically, coping and mastery have been defined in limited terms for the black male. Because he has been excluded from developing coping and mastery skills on the stages of the wider theater, his social competence may seem limited, which results in a vicious circle. Cool pose helps the black male cover up his lack of mastery and prevail in the face of unjust restrictions. It brings grace and flair to his interactions with others, including those who attempt to enforce those restrictions.

Pride and the Search for Meaning

Pride is the driving force behind the masking of cool pose. Although much was written about the rise of ethnic pride during the Black Power Movement and Black Revolution of the 1960s, little attention has been paid to how black males use pride as a means to enhance their personal social competence.

Pride is of colossal importance to black males. They engage in an unyielding drive toward the pursuit of pride. Pride, dignity, and respect hold such a high premium for black men that many are willing to risk anything for it, even their lives.

This need for pride develops early in the life of young black males. Black authors have written prideful speeches into their characters or autobiographies. In *Manchild in the Promised Land*, for example, Claude Brown recalls a trip to court after he had been hit by a bus. Even though his father is portrayed as an Uncle Tom, Brown dramatizes the importance of pride and respect from others in a young man's life. He would rather be in reform school—with his friends who have pride—than be free but without pride.

Cool As Protection

Playing it cool protects one's chance of survival and enhances self-esteem. Cool pose can be used as a form of protection against white authorities. The Man—police and other symbols of white authority—can be thrown off balance by a carefully staged cool performance. Cool pose serves as a guide for behavior under the kind of pressure that might occur during an encounter with the police or a boss. Phil says coolness gives him "a lead to what my next situation will be like. So I just can't come out in a bag [openly] all the time, because it don't pay, 'cause then if you do, then The Man will figure you out."

Cool pose helps ensure that The Man does not really know who the black male is, what he feels, or what he wants. It is an emotional shield that emanates from the mind, relates Phil: "That's right! Just use your mind, that's where it all starts at." Cool helps keep The Man off track. Phil says it is a way of controlling himself and protecting himself from being bothered, literally or psychologically: "You don't let him catch on to what you are doing. Just let him look at your work; if he sees something in your work that's not right, he's going to make you do a little bit more of everything. So, you have to use a cool to protect that."

The Negative Side of Being Cool

While the cool pose has positive effects, it has negative effects as well. A competent, prideful coolness may seem to elevate the cool male above his peers:

> The dilemma of the super-cool cat who revels in expressiveness is matched by the together guy in his insistence on doing his own thing. Both run the risk of alienating those who would have them adhere closely to peer group norms, to follow the crowd, to engage in deviant behavior which the cool guy often finds perilously and senselessly ridiculous."[1]

The masking central to cool pose also trains the black male in the art of self-deception. He may lose the ability to know his own feelings, to feel them keenly, or to express them to others when it is safe to do so. As Dworkin and Dworkin write, "the most tragic aspect of cool is that it exists not only as the handmaiden of survival in the ghetto, but that it has become a self-sustaining pattern independent of its original functional significance."[2]

Confounding of Therapy and Other Social Services

One of the major problems of attempting therapy or delivery of other social services with black males is self-disclosure. Most blacks do not come to therapy voluntarily, but are referred through the courts, social workers, medical personnel, and schools; once in therapy, they disclose less about themselves than does any other group.

Blacks still operate under a shield of distrust toward whites. And because they are inclined to define masculinity in terms of coolness, they are reluctant to share their deeper concerns with black or white members of the helping professions. In fact, they might even use the cool pose in therapy, through histrionic behaviors and strategic self-presentation.

Cool pose can be used to keep social service workers, mental health professionals, and therapists off guard. Some African-American males suspect that white counselors do not give them honest feedback, so they tell counselors what the counselors want to hear; they resort to playing games and faking it by adopting a cool pose.

Lack of self-disclosure on the client's part and lack of cultural sensitivity on the therapist's part, particularly with white therapists, thwarts attempts to solve problems with professional help and leads to frequent misdiagnosis. Many black males will not open up to white therapists because they view professionals as extensions of a society that contributed to the problems that brought them to therapy in the first place. They fear that by sharing their deepest feelings with white therapists they are giving more fuel to the enemy.

However, it is common for black males to resist self-disclosure with black male therapists as well. Expressing feelings is viewed as a sign of weakness or giving up; it is perceived as a loss of will and pride. Being honest could diminish respect, tarnish a reputation, and compromise manhood.

Distorted and Damaged Relationships

Expressing feelings and participating in mainstream activities may be defined as uncool in the male world, but this preoccupation with coolness is often problematic. Some black males have difficulty disclosing their deepest feelings even to those with whom they are expected to be closest: good friends, wives, mothers, fathers, girlfriends, and children. Keeping their guard up with white people makes it next to impossible to let their guard down for people they care about and who care about them.

This masking of true feelings interferes with establishing strong bonds with families and friends. Unfortunately for the black male who constantly puts himself under pressure to prove his manhood and is simultaneously unable to show or discuss his feelings and fears, the risk is very high for black-on-black crime, especially assault and homicide. The pent-up emotions born of frustration and disappointment may explode in aggressive acts against those who are closest to his daily life—other black people. The pervasive nature of coolness in many black males can have tragic consequences for their relationships with males and females, black or white.

BLACK MALES AND WHITE MALES. Many black males have become so conditioned to keeping their guard up against racism and social oppression that they tend to act cool much of the time, regardless of the circumstances. In this sense, cool pose is a "conditioned strength." What we call "the problem of selective indiscrimination" occurs because of the conditioned strength the black male has developed through his constant struggle with unyielding systems. This rigid and inflexible strength results in cool behaviors that seem automatic. The posturing of cool pose becomes such a major part of his psyche that even when white males are not present and are of no threat, the black male still operates in a "high cool gear." For some men being cool is never switched off.

Pettigrew cites William Faulkner's famous remark: "No white man understood [blacks] and never would so long as the white man compelled the black man to be first a [black] and only then a man, since this, the impenetrable dividing wall, was the black man's only defense and protection for survival."[3]

Sometimes that dividing wall is inappropriate, even destructive. In many situations the black male will assume a facade of strength at all costs, rather than "blow his front" and his cool. Cool pose may be used to show white males, "although you may have tried to hurt me time and time again, I can take it; if I am hurting or weak, I'll never let you know." This is also a way of saying, "I am strong and proud. I am a survivor." Failures and fears become the black man's secret. Being cool often represents his only safeguard against what he anticipates will be further mental or physical abuse.

Unfortunately, many black males are unable—because of anger, bitterness, and distrust toward whites—to mainstream or evolve other forms of consciousness. The cool front leads the black male to reject mainstream norms, aesthetics, mannerisms, values, etiquette, or information networks that could help him overcome the problems caused by white racism. His cool defense makes it extremely difficult for him to selectively let his guard down. He is impeded from showing affection for people he may really care about or people who may really care about him (including, ironically, nondiscriminating whites).

Another impact of cool pose on the black male's life is the negative interpretation of various cool behaviors by white males who observe blacks being emotionless, fearless, aloof, or macho. Not only do white males view these behaviors as mysterious and enigmatic rather than as cool, but they may interpret them to mean that black males are irresponsible, shiftless, unmotivated, and unconcerned. They might conclude that black males have an attitude problem; however, black males view these behaviors as being suave and debonair—cool.

These stereotypical interpretations by white males can lead them to reject or mistreat black males, which feeds into a downward spiral of frustration, anger, and distrust toward white males, often countered by the black male with a cool pose. This in turn feeds into further negative interpretations, and the vicious cycle of miscommunication between cultures and individuals is perpetuated.

BLACK MALES AND BLACK FEMALES. Cool behaviors may prevent black males from developing authentic relationships with women. Being cool is paradoxical because the behaviors that afford black males a semblance of social competence and control elsewhere in their lives are the same behaviors that ultimately help run their relationships with women aground.

An additional complexity arises: Black males often receive a double message from black females. Although many black females will argue that they dislike men who act and look cool, they often reward coolness.

Black females are sometimes turned on by or attracted to black males who act and look cool. Those males who do not act cool may suffer a heavy penalty of rejection. Some women are attracted to the urbane, emotionless, smooth, fearless, aloof, apparently masculine qualities of the cool pose. The cool man is an enigma—a challenge to females. Comments, such as the following, express the black female's ambivalence toward cool pose: "I just don't know where he's coming from"; "He won't show his feelings"; "He plays too many games"; "He's just too cool"; and "I just can't figure him out." Women's attraction to cool men reflects the old adage that "women don't want nice guys." The nice guy is not perceived as exciting or mysterious, but it is easier to fathom where the nice guy is coming from than it is to understand the cool male.

For black women who wish to develop intimate relationships with black men who act and look cool, it is the cool pose that attracts them. Ultimately, these cool behaviors may prevent couples from establishing strong, committed, and authentic relationships. The games and masks, the highly stylized expression of self that makes the cool male attractive, are the very same artifices that inhibit intimacy and genuine companionship.

When men believe that women want them to act in a cool manner, they actively display a cool pose in the courtship ritual. Distinctive rapping, strutting, cool stance, eye contact, gestures, and putting on the mask of masculinity are conjured up to attract desirable females. But cool behaviors cannot be turned on and off like a light switch. Not unlike his situation with the white man, it is often next to impossible for the black man to let his guard down for women, even when it could be to his advantage.

If he feels rejected, the black male may reject a woman rather than admit his hurt feelings. If he is frightened about sinking into the quagmire of unemployment and welfare checks, he may instead put on a bravado that dispels all appearances of fear. If he is sad about the fighting and deaths of his compatriots on the streets, he may mock her expressions of sadness. If she complains about his inadequacy in providing for her and their children, he may strike out in anger to cover his anguish. It may appear that he is emotionally drained, or dead.

Cool pose is potentially counterproductive when a man becomes obsessed with being cool just to win a woman's heart, only to find that the relationship sours when true intimacy does not materialize. He has become obsessed with being cool in order to obtain the rewards of courtship (sexual intimacy), but he fails to win genuine closeness and companionship because he has not allowed his deeper feelings to surface. (We discuss the black male as pimp for the women in his life in a later chapter.)

Generally speaking, use of cool behaviors is not as intensely central for black women as it is for black men. Just the same, it is our contention that some women use cool behaviors as a way to counter the attitudes and actions of cool black males. Some women may find it safer to be cool rather than expose their true feelings or emotions and risk the chance of being rejected, used, hurt, embarrassed, or insulted. They may play hard to get, which not only makes them more challenging, attractive, and mysterious but also gives them a greater sense of control and even an edge in the courting process. Black women use cool behaviors to help counter the effects of racism and social oppression, too.

While cool behaviors have advantages in the courting game, their simultaneous use by both parties can cause relationships to falter.

Inability to put one's feelings on the line prevents the development of sincere relationships between black males and females.

BLACK MALES AND BLACK MALES. The protective wall of cool pose, historically constructed against the forces of white racism, does not automatically crumble when black males interact with their brothers. The cool mask is a defense system that is not instantly turned on and off. It becomes a deep-seated part of the black male's personality, an integral part of the face he shows the world.

Cool pose shapes black male interactions by helping them express strength and toughness with strict discipline and conviction. Black males do not respect other black males who fail to display a strong image. Even if they do not feel strong on the inside, their deportment should announce strength, cool, and self-assurance on the outside.

Many black men have learned to live up to a harsh standard: real men are not involved with anyone or anything that is not cool. Adhering to this standard means that black men may have a hard time being down to earth with each other; they have to be cool, especially around the "fellas." Their behavior must follow an unyielding code of coolness in order to gain acceptance.

If a black man does not act in these prescribed ways, others are quick to ostracize and label him as corny, lame, or square. Coolness has become such an obsession with some black males that they may reject their brothers who do uncool things, such as camping, visiting a museum, or attending a concert, simply because such activities are seen as a sign of softness or hypersensitivity. (Fordham and Ogbu include them among activities that young blacks may see as "acting white.") Avoiding such activities—just to keep friends or to escape cruel labels—becomes essential to the cool pose. It also has the potential to thwart the enrichment and growth of a black youth because he avoids exposure to experiences that could help expand his personal, social, and political consciousness.

Suicide and the Search for Adolescent Identity

Coolness is a valued trait among many adolescent males. "Is he cool?" is frequently the first question one adolescent asks concerning another. Being cool is often the pivotal criterion for acceptance. Adolescents place onerous pressure on each other to conform to various kinds of cool behaviors. This pressure is amplified by the fact that adolescence is typically a period of confusion, ambivalence, emotional instability, identity confusion, and doubtful self-esteem. Being cool, rather than square, may help to enhance the adolescent's confidence and popularity.

Adolescents may become interested in certain cliques (athletics, greaseballs, preppies, punk rockers, nerds) on the basis of how cool the clique appears to be. Conversely, being accepted for membership in a clique depends on estimations of a young person's coolness. Those who fail to conform to the dictates of cool behavior may suffer rejection and narrowed access to coveted activities. Social isolation—the ultimate loneliness—and loss of self-esteem may contribute to the distressing rates of suicide among adolescents.

School Is Not Cool

Distancing themselves from uncool activities can have negative implications for how black males fare in the formal structures of school. Activities that are perceived as uncool are likely to include studying, going on field trips to museums, and relating positively to teachers. Avoiding such pursuits has the potential to stymie enrichment and education. The youth's growth is funneled through the narrow parameters of experiences deemed by his peer group and himself as cool.

Why does the black youth use cool pose to distance himself from school in the first place? Fordham and Ogbu offer a succinct analysis of black youths' collision with the contradictions of a discriminatory educational and work opportunity structure:

> First, white people provide them with inferior schooling and treat them differently in school; second, by imposing a job ceiling, white people fail to reward them adequately for their educational accomplishments in adult life; and third, black Americans develop coping devices which, in turn, further limit their striving for academic success.[4]

Even as young children, blacks learn that they are unlikely to be treated like white Americans, despite the claims of a democratic society, regardless of how hard they work or how bright they are. Fordham and Ogbu argue that, in the face of this cruel realization, blacks (as well as other subordinate minorities) develop an oppositional social identity and cultural frame of reference that results in a terrible dilemma: If the black child tries to conform to the expectations of white-dominated schools, he may be accused by his peers of "acting white" and may sense himself that he is losing his own culture—if he does not conform, he is labeled as lazy, slow, or difficult by adults who have significant reward power over him. To strive for academic success may result in being labeled a "brainiac" or even being physically assaulted by his peers; to resist the educational structure imposed by another culture may relegate him to the streets for life.

Cool pose is both the result of this dilemma, and helps to perpetuate the black youth's discomfort in the school environment. In "The Destruction of the Young Black Males," John Gaston cites a poem entitled "I Was Cool" that illustrates how these attitudes toward education can cause black males to fail in school:

They said the doors of opportunity were closing fast,
and all the signs said that the good times weren't going to last,
but that didn't bother me,
because I was cool.

My teachers kept trying to get me to learn read'n, writ'n and math,
talking about you need that stuff to make it down life's paths.
But I just looked at them, and laughed.
I said, "Ya'll might need to know that stuff, but not me, because I'm cool."

Them teachers was always getting on my case, and I told them
I knew that it was because of my race.
They just couldn't deal with me,
because they was square,
and I was cool.

I use to be so clean everybody would stop and stare,
'cause I was looking good with my curl free on my hair.
Hey, if you've got it, you've got it,
and I knew I was cool and looking good.
I didn't learn nothing in school, but they still let me pass.

I was sho gett'n ova,
even if I was at the bottom of my class.
But they still let me graduate from high school.
I definitely got ova!

But you can do that when you're cool.
After grad-u-ation I got clean and went to look for me a job.
I knew I was going to make me some long bread, buy me a new ride,
and stay clean and cool everyday!
I was definitely going to have everything my way!

But trying to read them job applications was far from a charm,
and I told the dude at the employment office I couldn't write too good,
'cause I'd hurt my arm.
But the look on his face told me that he didn't really believe that,
and the dude wasn't hardly impressed by my bad new hat.

Well to make a long story short, I finally got me a job,
but I don't get much pay,
and from the way things look its always gonna be that way.
I didn't learn much in school,
and you sure don't get paid much when all you can do is be cool.

If I could go back to school I'd learn all I could,
and every time I talk to other brothers I tell them they should.
I realize now that my future's not too bright,
and without education it's kinda hard to make things right.

You know now that I think about it,
maybe some of those teachers that I thought was getting on my case,
were actually trying to help me in the education race.
It sure hurts when I realize that with my abilities,
I could have been anything that I wanted to be,
if I had applied myself in school.
But instead of learning all I could in school,
I spent most of my time,
sitting in the back of the room,
looking good,
and being cool.[5]

Being Cool and Being Tough

Mancini, in *Strategic Styles,* identifies five distinct coping styles that
black males may use as a way to manage social, family, and environ-

mental pressures. She uses the character of Leroy, based on interviews with black teens in Roxbury, Boston, to illustrate the "tough-guy" style, which involves high levels of risk-taking, aggression, violence, or threats to use violence. This may lead the young male into delinquency, and later as an adult, criminality.

Mancini argues that the tough-guy style may be a by-product of family socialization. Some black males learn both affection and disapproval, especially toward their fathers, brothers, and other male relatives, by hitting, wrestling, fighting, tough playing, and punching. She notes that in Leroy's family the theme of violence was pronounced. When Leroy failed or disobeyed his parents, he would be "yelled at or pushed around." In families such as Leroy's, force is used as a normal means to handle interpersonal relationships. The norm of toughness may cause conflict and trouble with others outside the family, such as teachers, and may lead the youth to seek out peers who also are at home with tough behavior.

Other coping styles—conformity, withdrawal, conning, and being cool—can be used in tandem with toughness, as the situation dictates. And, as mentioned earlier, what a young school boy or adolescent thinks is cool may be interpreted in quite the opposite way by school administrators. Leroy gives a perfect example of this:

> We gotta wear ties at school. One day I didn't have mine on; I had it hangin' out my back pocket. The vice principal came, yankin' on my shoulder . . . he said, "put it on before I pick it out and hang it around your neck." So I told him to try it. He took the tie out, tried to get it around my neck, and I snatched it and pushed him; he leaned back on the table and flipped right over it.

Leroy's attempt to dress in a cool (albeit defiant) fashion leads him into a confrontation, which escalates into the use of force on both sides, and Leroy's expulsion for the day.

Cool, tough, risk-taking behaviors may be influenced by two defenses: reaction formation and denial. Reaction formation means that young black youths are frightened and frustrated by school but act as though they are in control. Such behaviors are often an unconscious protest against the dominant society, as symbolized by teachers and school administrators. Instead of expressing bitterness and anger directly, black males twist those feelings into the opposite—the cool pose. Denial of their true feelings may help black males pretend that white hostility and discrimination have no effect on them.

Delinquency and Gangs

Gangs and delinquency epitomize the pursuit of masculinity through toughness and cool. The gang member's frustration develops out of a long history of social and economic neglect. He epitomizes the frustrated black male in America. In 1987, the black teenage unemployment rate was 34 percent. In some metropolitan areas, it is as high as 70 percent. And, in most major urban areas in the United States—home for many black youths—recreation, health, and social centers are hard to find. Many youths are angry and embittered by the social wasteland of neglect and isolation created by centuries of second-class status and ghettoization.

Joining a gang is a way to organize and make sense of the marginal world of the inner city neighborhood. It is a way to direct anger and create excitement and entertainment. The gang can become a family that offers belonging, pride, respect, and empowerment that may be absent in the home and denied by society. The gang member is symbolically stating, "I may not be able to depend on you, society, but I can count on these guys."

For black males who have been locked out of the social and economic mainstream, running with a gang can be a form of social achievement, as can engaging in fortuitous violence. Staying cool under threat of apprehension, fast-talking his way out of tight situations, or garnering the affection of peers and girls as he swaggers through perilous encounters with The Man is a heady way to live. Involvement in drugs, fighting, stealing, gambling, drinking, drugs, hustling, or pimping can enhance flagging self-esteem. Dignity and recognition are bound up with the immediate rewards of money and material goods. Unfortunately, trouble, uncertainty, violence, murder, and arrest are the by-products. This account by Leroy is illustrative:

> [Trouble] just happens. We go outside, you know, when I have a fight, go places . . . we go to a party or whatever, or a lounge . . . and a fight starts, and we all grab bottles, you know, and we just go out looking for trouble. That's with the whities . . . bump into persons and knock

them down for fun, try and upset cars, tear off car antennas for no reason at all. That's trouble right there.

By age 21, Leroy has been implicated in two cases of manslaughter and several robberies. He feels no guilt and claims that running with his gang is fun and exciting: "Me and these other fellows would gather around with Joe, get drunk, go out, start some shit . . . Have a little party. Fight a while. Me and him have a little beef, got busted up and what not, went to jail . . . from then on I kept on gettin' in trouble."

Not all gangs are as violent or as involved in drinking, but the high-risk, confrontational street life is exhilarating for many. Black gang members become anything but Ellison's invisible men. They make themselves visible through acts of anger and defiance, pride and protest, and solidarity and deviance. The resulting power and entertainment can be seductive.

African-American gang members have their own rules and culture. They are consumed with symbols that identify and promote a masculine cultural display: distinctive handshakes, hairstyles, stance, walks, battle scars, turf wars, hand signals, language, and nicknames. Clothing can signify gang membership and solidarity: baseball caps, jackets, sweat suits, bandannas, hairnets, and leather sneakers. Use of certain colors or the wearing of gold chains and other special jewelry also signify gang loyalty.

Countless masculinity rituals are used to express brotherhood. The PGBs, a Los Angeles gang, require potential members to engage in a ritual called "jump in." The aspirant must buy a pair of khaki pants, "sag" the waist, and "put on that look." Then he must choose three PGB members and jump in to fight them *en masse*. If he is still standing after ten minutes, he is in the gang. Fighting not only serves as a membership entrance fee, but the aspirant also gains prestige, respect, and status in the eyes of his peers.

Gang violence can be used to achieve symbolic gains: drive-by shootings, the placing of a black wreath on a person's door (serving notice that the gang wants to execute that person), graffiti messages scribbled on walls to communicate a gang's intent, or a "Columbia necktie" displayed at the site of someone's death (a murder victim's throat is cut, and the tongue is pulled through the cut). For example, when a gang in Los Angeles spray paints the police murder code (187) on a building, it means they are making a death threat.[6]

According to Squitieri, gang violence and assaults have increased not only in giant cities the size of Los Angeles, but even in small towns, such as Tyler, Texas. There, one judge has seen a shift in gang crimes from burglary and theft to aggravated assault, rape, and attempted murder. She claims to be able to tell the difference between gang and nongang members by their faces and eyes: Gang members show no emotion.

Statistics support her impression that gang violence has proliferated and become more serious. In Los Angeles 750 gangs claim up to 100,000 members total. Since 1977, gang homicides in this beleaguered city have increased from 168 to a 1989 high of 515. As is true nationally, crimes against persons have increased at a much higher rate than crimes against property: Since 1984, gangs in Los Angeles have killed over 2,000 individuals; the gang-related incidence of attempted murder is up by over 50 percent; assaults are up by 25 percent; and robberies have increased by 12 percent.[7]

Although many gang members attend school, hard-core youth are not likely to be dissuaded from magnified masculine/violent attitudes by sitting in a classroom for a few hours each day. Many attend school irregularly anyway, and when they do, gang violence is brought into the schools with them in the form of assaultive behavior, possession of weapons, substance abuse, and theft. The usual punishment—suspension from school—feeds into dropping out, which in turn has devastating implications.

Risk-taking delinquent or gang activities are often self-destructive to black males. The search for power may actually end in total loss of power with their apprehension, incarceration, or death. Until we provide more opportunities for potential black gang members, the problem will only worsen.

Compromised Race Relations

The recent prominence of such groups as the Aryan Nation, the revival of the Ku Klux Klan movement, and the Forsyth County and Howard Beach racial incidents are clear indications that race relations remain strained between blacks and whites. Understanding cool behaviors has important implications for improving race relations.

In *Black and White Styles in Conflict*, Kochman argues that a gulf exists between black and white styles. Black styles are more often characterized by expressive and performance behavior: high-stimulus, spontaneous, intuitive, improvisational, emotional, rhythmic, assertive, confrontational, direct, and animated. White behavior is more often seen as low-stimulus: dispassionate, nonchallenging, and impersonal. While blacks are more interested in expressing than controlling their impulses, whites value self-restraint, understatement, and diffusion of intense situations.

When white people observe black males displaying cool pose, being aloof and seemingly fearless, they may see them as mysterious and imperturbable. But they may also see them as irresponsible, shiftless, and unmotivated. What the black male regards as cool, the white person may define as an attitude problem.

These crossed definitions of interpersonal interaction have led many whites to react negatively to black males and to mistreat them; and they have led many black males to resent "whitey" for rejecting or misunderstanding him. For example, Phil believes that black males have to use cool in order to "get over" white people:

> They better use it! If you don't use it, you ain't going to get nowhere. You're going to find that out. You got to be cool but you've got to get them on your side to a point. I mean, you don't have to be no "Tom." No, you ain't got to go up there and kiss the man's butt. You just go in there and deal with him.

Fear and anxiety mark interracial contacts, especially those that occur between strangers, at night, or on the urban streetscape. Attempts to reach out across racial barriers are often met with hostility on both sides. Misunderstandings arise from misinterpreted verbal and nonverbal cues and the enormous power of stereotypes. The resentment of both whites and blacks that naturally arises from feeling misunderstood feeds back into the misunderstandings.

Since cool pose contributes to distorted relationships on all fronts, it is important to explore its origins. Clearly, it is a response to dominance; ironically, it may also perpetuate dominance. What are the wellsprings of cool pose in the history of black males in Africa and America?

He's not honest. No, he's not himself. A cool person to me—I've met a lot of cool guys—on the outside they're not what they really are like on the inside. They've got like a barrier: "Oh, this is what I am, you know, I've got this, I've got that, and I love ya." It's not true, they're not themselves; they want to be what everybody else is.

—Sue, 26

A cool person is a person who is trying to be cool when he's not. Sometimes it means he's a calm person, or a person who is naturally himself.

—Sonny, 17

5

The Genesis of Black Masking

> Got one mind for white folks to see,
> 'Nother for what I know is me;
> He don't know,
> He don't know my mind, when he sees me laughing
> Just laughing to keep me from crying.
> —R. Ames

A repertoire of black styles, including cool pose, has sprung from a unique fusion of African heritage with the legacy of a ruthless slave system within the country that eventually freed blacks. In this chapter, we trace the elements of cool and masking in West African culture, through the slave period in America, and to the contemporary condition of blacks.

West African Culture: A Different Metaphor

Traditional West African culture has had a colossal impact on African-American culture. Recognition of this cultural imprint may provide valuable insights into how expressive life-style behaviors evolve in African-Americans.

African culture features spiritualism, expressiveness, and spontaneity. According to African belief systems, the universe is a vitalistic, spiritual life force—an organic system in harmony with nature. By comparison, the Euro-American belief system centers on materialism and mastery over nature. Boykins calls these opposites the *organic metaphor* and the *mechanistic metaphor*. The organic metaphor emphasizes expressive movement; the mechanistic metaphor centers on impulse control. African culture emphasizes interconnectedness and communalism; Euro-American culture values separateness and independence.

Emotion versus reason, natural time versus clock time, oral culture versus print culture: These contrasts go further. In African culture, expressive individualism and communalism are compatible ideals. While possessions belong to the community at large, uniqueness is valued. Euro-American culture, on the other hand, forces possessiveness and individualism to live in the same boat.

Boykins identifies nine interrelated dimensions that have filtered from West African culture into African-American culture, influencing the development of expressive behaviors in black men:

Spirituality—an approach to life as being essentially vitalistic rather than mechanistic, with the conviction that nonmaterial forces influence people's everyday lives;

Harmony—the notion that one's fate is interrelated with other elements in the scheme of things, so that humankind and nature are harmonically conjoined;

Movement—an emphasis on the interweaving of movement, rhythm, percussiveness, music, and dance, all of which are taken as central to psychological health;

Verve—a propensity for relatively high levels of stimulation and for action that is energetic and lively;

Affect—an emphasis on emotions and feelings, together with a special sensitivity to emotional cues and a tendency to be emotionally expressive;

Communalism—a commitment to social connectedness, which includes an awareness that social bonds and responsibilities transcend individual privilege;

Expressive individualism—the cultivation of a distinctive personality and proclivity for spontaneous, genuine personal expression;

Oral tradition—a preference for oral/aural modes of communication, in which both speaking and listening are treated as performances, and cultivation of oral virtuosity—the ability to use alliterative, metaphorically colorful, graphic forms of spoken language; and

Social time perspective—an orientation in which time is treated as passing through a social space rather than a material one, and in which time can be recurring, personal, and phenomenological.

Each of these dimensions—spirituality, verve, movement, harmony, emotion, orality, expressive individualism, personal time, and communalism—becomes manifest in a single expression: being cool.

The Roots of Cool in African Culture

Being cool has played an important role in the historical, social, and cultural development of black people. Coolness was central to the culture of many ancient African civilizations. Cultural anthropologist John Janzen dates the phenomenon of cool in Africa back to at least 2000–3000 B.C. He believes that coolness was expressed in oral culture, character building, artwork, linguistics, dance, initiation rituals, warrior cults, mating rituals, and the concept of health.

Art historian Robert Farris Thompson writes of the historical importance of cool. He believes it originated in Nigeria in the first half of the fifteenth century. *Ewuare* was the name given to the person crowned king of the Nigerian empire, Benin. The name literally meant "it is cool." In the same century, a Yoruba ruler from Ilobi, in what is now southern Egabado, took the name *Oba tio tutu bi asun*, which means "Cool-and-Peaceful-As-the-Native-Herb-Osun."

In the sixteenth century, the same name was awarded to an Ijebu Yoruba king. The Yoruba exhibited "itutu," a more mystical version of cool. Thompson writes of the "equilibrium and poetic structure" of traditional Yoruba dances. The frozen facial expressions worn by contemporary Yoruba who perform these dances express cool as a patient outlook and collectedness of mind.

As an ancient and indigenous part of black culture, the idea of cool bears a spiritual meaning: sense of control, symmetry, correct presentation of self, and sophistication. Coolness is a part of character— *ashe*. To exhibit grace under pressure is akin to exuding a royal demeanor. A noble confidence and mystic coolness of character, ashe reveals an inner spirituality and peace that marks the strongest of men. True ashe is a reflection of true inner strength, just as cool pose is often the mask that hides inner turmoil and anxiety. That mask became a matter of survival, as well as of spirituality, during the grim transfer of Africans to the Americas via enslavement.

The Legacy of Slavery: An Exquisite Sensibility

Until a mere thirty years ago, African-Americans have been an enslaved people, an internally colonized people, and a ghettoized people, all within the system that declares them now to be free and equally competitive. The legacy of enforced passivity and negative identity will not easily be shed, like the dried, thin skin of a cocoon, in a matter of a few decades—perhaps not even generations. This is a wound that runs deep and hurts profoundly.

Ironically, although blacks are a highly visible minority in terms of skin color and other physical features, they have also been rendered invisible in many ways. Early in American history they, like women, were considered chattel, property, soul-less, or animals. Subsequently, they were left out of the larger American picture of freedom and self-determination by being defined as mentally and morally inferior. Blacks have been portrayed as watermelon-loving, innocent, lazy, or simple, which in turn has fed into their systematic exclusion from the most fundamental opportunity structures that stand at the heart of the American way: education, homeownership, and upward mobility through career advancement.

Although most minority groups have suffered through some period of racism and discrimination and have developed similar defensive postures to some extent, no other group has experienced such systematic degradation within our political boundaries. Blacks in America have endured a far more pervasive and long-lasting oppression that is rivaled only by the social annihilation of blacks in South Africa's cruel system of apartheid.

And, of course, enslavement of blacks was so central to earlier American life that the country was torn asunder by the Civil War, which was fought in part to preserve slavery. The guilt and shame, pain and torment of living through slavery, the debate over its moral and political merits and the aftermath of freedom, have been experienced by no other American minority group. Only native Americans have come close to the legally sanctioned and persistent debasement experienced on this soil by African-Americans, and their rates of social pathology reflect that sad history as well.

Lyman and Scott write that blacks in America have a precarious status that has resulted in a subculture—constructed around the phenomenon of cool—that cuts across social rank. For those who live in the shadow of slavery, their most prized possession may be personal character, or ashe. Creativity and imagination are the only limits in establishing a personal status based on posturing, prevarication, and coolness.

One result of pervasive and prolonged oppression is that blacks have developed an exquisite sensibility to white cues. Many have become proficient at concealing their emotions. In the slavery period of the old South and later in the harder-to-read North, the black male learned through almost daily experience that, somehow, he had been assigned a restricted role. He learned to play that role with a finesse and artistry that became part of his culture. Around whites he mastered the art of concealment, his mask constructed, as Kochman observes, of innocence and ignorance, childishness and humility, and obedience and deference. If he let that mask down in the white South, he risked psychological and even physical brutality; later, if he let it down in the North, he risked social rejection and loss of employment as well.

The isolation of African-Americans from African culture since the days of the slave trade and the isolation of blacks from whites throughout American history have generated unique nonverbal behaviors that contribute to cool. Symbolic gestures indicating self-preservation, camaraderie, distrust, and bitterness have functioned to express otherwise forbidden feelings and also to entertain other blacks. The specific gestures and symbols change from time to time, but their purpose remains the same. African-American culture is a dynamic, evolving expression that is often elevated to the form of art.

The Black Mask

With the advent of slavery, it is likely that using the mask as a coping style became widespread among black males. African-

American women began to wear some of the same masks in response to the burdens of racial oppression, but the styles of black males appear to have become more crystallized. Perhaps males posed a greater menace to whites, especially as perceived threats to white female sexuality, and so drew harsher reactions.

Perkins reminds us that if we are to appreciate the nature of black life-styles, we must accept this key fact: Blacks have emerged from an atypical environment. The emergent coping styles have been essential to black survival in an environment of servitude and ghettoization. Impression management—the ability to be flexible in presentation of self, to role-play according to the expectations of an audience that has superior reward power, to decipher meanings of the dominant group—has made the difference between those who survived and those who did not.

The masking behaviors that black males have devised to hide their pain and protect themselves from further insult are extensive and unique. Even though masking is unnecessary in particular situations or with certain people, nevertheless it is the proud signature of a group struggling to create its own identity in spite of deadening subjugation.

Historically, the black mask of roles, facades, shields, fronts, and gaming helped to ensure survival. This created what Nielson calls a ubiquitous "curtain of invisibleness." Northern whites felt the curtain but were generally unable to penetrate it. Regardless of class, blacks knew that donning the masked role was the safest course. They played to the expectations of the powerful white audience.

Children learned early to suppress their natural feelings of fear, hatred, or confusion. Fitting on the mask was a part of growing up black and an extension of the instinct to survive. Faked friendliness, aloof obedience, and Uncle Tom solicitousness were responses to the casting calls of slavery period whites. Whites wanted the blacks who lived and worked close to them to play one role— affable compliance—and to play it well. Those expectations wove a persistent thread through interracial relations in this country. Myrdal, in his searing analysis, *An American Dilemma*, calls this the "tyranny of expectancy."

The facade has been part of a survival kit for life in a racist country. Ridley writes that the black male has learned to accommodate The Man by orchestrating his speech, intonation, gesture, and facial expressions to produce an acceptable appearance. This performance is constructed out of fear, respect for the enemy's superior power, and a will to survive. Ridley says blacks became competent actors who developed a keen sense of what might satisfy whites, especially authority figures. This helped blacks stay out of trouble and get out of trouble.

Yet even in sliding into the mask that would appease whites and playing the roles that whites expected, blacks did not achieve freedom from harm, oppression, or stereotyping degradation. Novelist James Baldwin writes about the complexities and power of masking and role-playing. He knew that whites foolishly interpreted the mask as an authentic performance, so he played "endless and sinister variations" on the role they had assigned. Baldwin calculated that whites would never call his hand; he talks about moving into sensitive situations with superbly tuned perceptions, pride, and contempt for the game.

The black mask is similar to what others have called a front or persona. The black male develops complex game plans to maintain his front. The mask or front, which is fused from an amalgam of verbal, physical, and psychological elements, changes according to what the audience wants. This is the safest mask of all. The chameleon-like recasting of masks according to audience expectations marks the black actor's most heroic—and circumspect—performance.

The black male's psychological stance, then, is protective, cautious, and secretive in the face of the overwhelming power and advantage of white people and white institutions. The animosity he feels whenever he travels in white worlds is translated into the cue for donning the mask, playing to the crowd, and erecting the invisible wall. The mask is fabricated to defend against his fear of total disintegration and loss of self. This is a performance that runs in the family; it was passed down through generations who lived in traditional Africa during the times when ashe (cool pride) was a noble quality, distorted by slavery, and transformed into the daily mask of survival in contemporary American society.

Black Acting

The impervious mask often adopted by blacks in relation to whites facilitates internal balance. As with an actor who has played the same role night after night, the lines may become automatic. The phenomenon of black acting has been recognized by observers for many decades. Richard Wright, in *White Man Listen!*, defines the masking behavior of American blacks as a kind of "black acting" that entails hiding deepest reactions from those who have the power to punish them. This does not imply that blacks are dishonest or duplicitous: "They are about as honest as anybody else, but they are cautious, wise, and do not wish to bring undue harm upon themselves."[1]

In fact, blacks act to the degree that they perceive white hostility. Black acting implies regulating one's manner and tone of voice in a perfected system of concealment. Hammond argues that because black males seldom reveal their feelings, others have difficulty understanding their behavior. Cloaked feelings mean that those who think they know black men well may not even have grazed the tip of the iceberg.

Reed Smith, in his early article "The Unknowable Negro," sees the black man as a "superlative actor and pantomimist" who lets whites see only what he wants them to see. Contrary to the old adage, the black man says what he may not mean and feels what he does not say. Smith believes that no other group is "more secretive" and none so puzzling to psychologists.

Similarly, in *Black Ethos*, Nielson suggests that many blacks are "theatrical," adopting in daily interaction with whites the voices and gestures associated with mimes: "I saw Africano, back of the smoke screen of his constitutional guarantee, all wispy and valueless, facing . . . the necessity of adapting himself to a harsh and often lethal environment."[2]

American black poetry and folk songs have also documented such themes of discretion, disguise, and concealment as playing it cool, masking, and black acting. An example is this classic poem by Paul Lawrence Dunbar, entitled "We Wear the Mask":

> We wear the mask that grins and lies,
> It hides our cheeks and shades our eyes,
> This debt we pay to human guile: With
> torn and bleeding hearts we smile, And
> mouth with myriad subtleties.
> Why should the world be overwise,
> In counting all our tears and sighs?
> Nay, let them only see us while
> We wear the mask.

We smile, but, O' great Christ, our cries
To thee from tortured souls arise.
We sing, but oh the clay is vile
Beneath our feet, and long the mile;
But let the world dream otherwise,
We wear the mask.[3]

Shucking

Shucking is another unique form of masking black males have used successfully since slavery. Shucking is a communication style that conforms to racial stereotypes yet cognitively rejects them at the same time. Stanback and Pearce define shucking as talk and physical movements that construct a temporary guise or facade designed to accommodate The Man. Shucking produces, in the moment of an encounter, whatever appearance The Man would find acceptable.

Kochman says the function of shucking is to work on "members of the establishment" in a way that will result in the black male gaining some advantage. It is a defensive performance that promotes a stereotypical image that is bought by the audience but disbelieved by the performer. In this sense, shucking is another form of black acting.

Black Humor: "I'm Still Here, Daddy-O, I'm Still Here"

Black humor also provides a way to establish visibility and legitimacy. It is yet another strategy that black males have used for surviving dominance. Black humor was born out of slavery as a way to maintain sanity and integrity. To be able to laugh at whites and the conditions of black oppression allowed black people to express deeper truths with impunity and with a healing effect. They could comment obliquely or absurdly on deadly serious issues that affected their daily lives: lynchings, violence, rape, murder, debasement, suspicion, false accusations, social barricades, and frustrations.

Jokes allowed blacks to feel superior and seize the upper hand, if only in words. For example, LeVine describes the wit of the "human trickster tales" told during and after slavery. Black humor was the vehicle for mocking white pretension and hypocrisy:

Indeed, nothing more effectively burlesqued the entire notion of ownership in human beings than the incessantly told story of the slave who was caught killing and eating one of his master's pigs and who mockingly rationalized his act by arguing that since both the animal and the slave were the master's possession nothing was lost: "Yes, suh, Massa, you got less pig now but you sho' got more nigger."[4]

This popular joke carried logical thought to its most absurd conclusion to beat whites at their own game. Laughter helped assuage the pain, subtle humor helped comprehend a social arrangement that lacked any universal moral logic, and jokes helped release the tension of hatred.

Not surprisingly, black humor often rests on the reversal of racial roles, with blacks suddenly elevated to a superior position and whites tricked or humiliated, flattened into subjugation. Jokes disguise hostility and aggression just enough to make them safe. Such tendentious jokes are best made against those who claim authority over others. The jokes then represent a form of rebellion, as well as of liberation.

The liberation of feelings that were otherwise forbidden expression brought relief to slaves and still provides exceedingly poignant moments of pleasure for contemporary blacks. As in all drama, the juxtaposition of comedy and drama, laughter and tears, is both startling and refreshing. It holds great survival value, for to cry always or to grieve always about one's losses and hardships breeds depressive paralysis. Humor grounded in reality makes reality seem more bearable.

A folkloric hero who epitomizes black humor, durability, and the strength of black males is Jesse B. Simple. Simple is a fictional underemployed black male living in Harlem in the 1940s and 1950s. He is the creation of Langston Hughes, who used gallows humor to reflect black life in white America. In this passage, Simple is recuperating from pneumonia. He places his illness in the context of a myriad of routine tragedies:

"Not only am I half dead right now from pneumonia, but everything else has happened to me! I have been cut, shot, stabbed, run over, hit by a car, and tromped on by a horse. I have been robbed, fooled, deceived, two-timed, double-crossed, dealt seconds, and right near blackmailed—but I am still here."

"You're a tough man," I said.

"I have been fired, laid off, and last week given an indefinite vacation, also Jim Crowed, segregated, barred out, insulted, eliminated, called black, yellow, and red, locked in, locked out, locked up, also left holding the bag. I have been caught in the rain, caught in raids, caught short with my rent, and caught with another man's wife. In my time I have been caught, but I am still here!"

"You have suffered," I said.

"Suffered!" cried Simple. "My mamma should have named me Job instead of Jess Simple. I have been underfed, underpaid, undernourished, and everything but undertaken. I been bit by dogs, cats, mice, rats, poll parrots, fleas, chiggers, bedbugs, granddaddies, mosquitoes, and gold-toothed woman."

"Great day in the morning!"

"That ain't all," said Simple. "In this life I have been abused, confused, misused, accused, false-arrested, tried, sentenced, paroled, black-jacketed, beat, third-degreed, and near about lynched."

"Anyhow, your health has been good—up to now," I said.

"Good health nothing," objected Simple, waving his hands, kicking off the cover, and swinging out of bed. "I done had everything from flat feet to a flat head. Why, man, I was born with measles! Since then I had smallpox, chickenpox, whooping cough, croup, appendicitis, athlete's foot, tonsillitis, arthritis, backache, mumps, and a strain—but I am still here, Daddy-O, I'm still here!"

"Having survived all that, what are you afraid of, now that you are almost over pneumonia?"

"I'm afraid," said Simple, "I will die before my time."[5]

Inversion

Another mask that the black male has used with success is inversion, which is based on the premise that even though he cannot disguise the color of his skin, he can certainly disguise the meaning behind his speech. Inversion turns the tables, reversing the meaning of stereotypical images in a way that befuddles white interpretations of communication. Holt says this enables blacks to deceive and manipulate whites without fear of penalty.

Inversion allows the expression of true feelings in masked form. This type of humor affords self-expression and helps build solidarity among blacks, who see through the manipulation their brothers "put over" on whites. Holt describes inversion as behavior that whites would perceive as inappropriate, but which at the same time elevates "whitey" to a false status. Praise and ridicule are woven into the same interaction. The police patrolman becomes "chief," the ex-private is elevated to "captain," and the ex-captain is promoted to "colonel." The flattery is so overblown that whites would be reluctant to correct it.

This traps the white victim through an exaggerated, yet unrealistic, admiration that in fact undercuts his authority in the subtlest of ways. To attempt such an undercutting openly would be far too dangerous. Inversion is a creative practice that uses The Man's own language against him; it is a mockery that wards off debasement by that same language.

For the black mask to drop, the stage must be altered. Props, lighting, scenery, parts, scripts, and rewards must be completely reconstituted into a new production. In many ways the mask was highly effective for the black male as he made the passage from Africa to a not-so-brave new world. It also ensnared him.

The cool person shouldn't be extreme on either side. Not too materialistic, not too lame. There should be a little bit of both, then you can be regarded as cool, or whatever the term is at that time. But if it's too extreme, then you wouldn't be given the respect and attention that potentially you could get. A bit of materialistic, a bit of attitude.

—Joe, 20

It's all peer pressure on the part of the young folks. No one wants to become a dumb ass. Everyone wants to hear, oh, he's fresh, he's got values, he's a nice guy, he looks like this . . . the pressure is there.

—Dave, 35

6

The Expressive Life-Style

*Ah, man, look here—that's just the style. You know, man, black men
just like to be-bop-bop down the street. The black man got rhythm. See,
that is what the white man is trying to pick up! See, the brothers and I
say it's just a style.*

—Phil

Black acting, humor, inversion, and shucking are all forms of acting that spring from the unique history of African-Americans and,
in turn, contribute to the cool pose that so many contemporary
black males have mastered. The expressive life-style is one way
many black males play it cool. Styling, performing, and other types
of creative interpersonal expression accentuate the self, help obtain
gratification, release pent-up aggression and anger, and express
pride for self and race. The expressive life-style is entertainment. It
is also an important coping mechanism.

The Spontaneous Self

This expressive, artistic life-style is spontaneous and individualistic
in nature. Creative interpretation marks the black male's uniqueness
as a human being. As Parker notes, blacks have not given up on
their humanism or their feelings of uniqueness within the context of
a shared experience.

This leads to a quality of spontaneity and openness—to a certain aliveness and animation—that marks black style. White identifies six recurring patterns in the expressive behaviors that many
African-American men use: emotional vitality, realness, resilience,
interrelatedness, the value of direct experience, and distrust and

deception. These themes symbolize the cultural flavor of the black experience.

Being Alive

Rainwater describes the expressive life-style as a strategy that makes the African-American male interesting and attractive. By making himself an interesting person, the black male can elicit the responses he desires from others. The strain of living in a relatively hopeless world inspires him to find ways of announcing that he is, in fact, very much alive.

The cool, expressive life-style is not only a way of getting around dispiriting blocks to legitimate means of creative expression; it also acts as a way for the black male to accentuate or display his interior, deeper self. It is a way to be noticed, to draw attention, and to affirm his very essence. This helps to neutralize or counter the effects of racism and the threat of a static existence. The expressive life-style is an overt and often flamboyant way in which African-American males fashion an external image, stabilize self-esteem, and obtain gratification.

The expressive life-style is very important to African-Americans, especially males. As we discussed in chapter 5, blacks have been forced into conciliatory and often demeaning positions in American culture. But there is nothing conciliatory about the expressive life-style. This dynamic vitality can be detected even in stereotypical roles, such as the maid, Hattie McDaniel, in *Gone with the Wind* or affable servant Bill "Bojangles" Robinson in Shirley Temple movies. The black person's need for creative self-expression knows no bounds and is the passion that invigorates an otherwise demeaning life in white America.

The expressive life-style transforms the mundane to the sublime and makes the routine spectacular. It is a dynamic rather than a static art form characterized by such new aesthetics as rap music, "the cabbage patch dance," and breakdancing. Expressive behavior proclaims: "White man, this is my turf. You can't outdo me here."

The African-American male's relative impotence in the political and corporate worlds is countered with a potency and verve that borders on the spectacular, especially in athletic competition, entertainment, and the pulpit. Through the virtuosity of a performance, he tips socially imbalanced scales in his favor. "See me, touch me, hear me, but white man, you can't copy me" is his subliminally assertive message.

Expressiveness may be displayed by black males in a myriad of ways. Speech becomes rapping. Nicknames furnish unique identities. Clothes and hairstyles take on a special panache. Walk, stance, gestures, and handshakes become the distinctive idiom of everyday encounters. Music and sports become stages for the expressive style, from the high soprano voices of some black male singers to the personal signature many have affixed to sporting events. Dancing approaches art: The choreographed cool dance steps of soul music are rivaled by the more recent breakdancing and other new dance forms.

The Style Factor

As the word implies, "style" permeates expressive life-style behaviors. Black males have learned in the streetscape of their neighborhoods to walk, talk, and act in ways that advertise coolness. The lessons of the street make it possible to survive in the street. A public persona evolves that allows each male his own stylistic signature or "rep." Abrahams claims that exhibitionism permeates black male life-styles. It can even become more important than life itself. Style is the person; the person is his style. Style makes a statement about how he wishes to be perceived.

Mancini says that each youth develops a "strategic style" that marks his typical encounters with the people who are important to him on an everyday basis: being cool, tough, conformist, conning, or together; style expresses the way he defines masculinity. His strategic style is the "characteristic way the individual handles himself, others, and his physical/cultural world, based on the meaning he has come to attach to himself and others . . ."[1] Strategic style is in flux and is open to constant negotiation, depending on the audience to whom he is playing, but it is also a patterned way of constructing a manageable interpersonal environment. Style is not simply a reaction to cues given by others in a particular interaction, but is a person's way of acting, creating, and redefining his self *in relation to* others:

Strategic style is the way a person deals with the definitions prevailing in the cultures most salient to him. It includes the way in which he defines situations in his own right, and the information about himself he expresses or "gives off."[2]

Style includes attitudes, assumptions, and feelings about self and others, as they are expressed in language, dress, and nonverbal behavior. Folb elaborates further:

> Whether it's your car, your clothes, your young body, your new hairdo, your jewelry, you style it. The word "style" in vernacular usage means to show off what you've got. And for teenagers with little money and few actual possessions, showing off what you do have takes on increased importance. As one youth put it, "It's identity. It's a big ego trip."[3]

Style of this consistency is generally not seen among white males; African-Americans have had years to forge a unique style out of the crucible of oppression. Some white men may be cool, but black males do not believe that it is the same type of cool. In fact, white males who try to use the cool pose may be perceived by black males as corny. In a conversation with Majors, Phil explains: "They don't have the style, man. Who wants to walk around and say, h-e-y g-u-y?" In trying to look cool, whites may simply come across as awkward. They try to talk slang and act cool, he says, but "it's stupid!" Phil imitates how a white male might attempt to be cool:

> "B-r-o-t-h-e-r, w-h-a-t h-a-p-p-i-n'?" All that, ol' wild, off-the-wall kind of talk. I sit back and watch these white dudes who try to be cool and try to dress like blacks. Some of them can and some of them can't. The ones that can't, you can tell it because they are all out of proportion. They stand out like a sore thumb. They try to be hip and can't.

In fact, it is a source of pride that white males who try to talk, walk, and dance like black youths often cannot pull it off. They look foolish.

Nonverbal Styling

Historically, when African-Americans expressed their feelings openly, they were often severely punished; they had to learn to use expressions that would minimize or avoid punishment and harm.

Nonverbal expression has been widely cited as a key feature of African-American expression since slavery.[4]

The Black Power Movement of the late 1960s and early 1970s reflected a period of symbolism when handshakes, walking styles, and gestures became the trusted symbol of solidarity, masculinity, anger, and struggle. Defiance and unity, protest and brotherhood, were announced in the donning of an African *dashiki* or the sporting of an Afro ("natural") hairstyle. This was intended to make an ideological statement that was contrary to the trend of earlier decades when blacks spent enormous amounts of time and money making their hair straight ("processed"). By the late 1960s, the process or "do" was considered demeaning and "wanting to look white"—lacking in essential racial pride and self-esteem.

Some popular contemporary hairstyles are the shag (shorter on top, longer in back) and the flattop (usually cropped short on the sides). The cool male may sport multiple hair parts or a tail (a longer, braided piece of hair along the back of the neck). The fade displays hair cut at different lengths on top and shorter around the ears. In addition, the punk rock movement has influenced black hairstyles: spikes, buzzcuts, mohawk cuts, and dyed hair are occasionally seen. Braids are also in vogue. Jeri curls and perms alter natural curl. And some black males make use of the natural wavy-look hairstyle: Hair is cut close to the scalp, and before bed, is smoothed with a pomade and covered with a stocking cap to bring out a wavy look.[5]

Nonverbal styling includes expression through walking, body stance, handshakes, and eyework that communicates in a controlled and purposive fashion. Facial expressions are also important nonverbal cues for understanding people in any culture. Ironically, for blacks, the masking of facial expressions is just as crucial.

The conspicuous and expressive nature of the African-American male's walk has become a way to announce his presence, to accentuate his self, and to broadcast his prideful power. Those in the black community who choose not to use this culturally specific behavior may be subject to ridicule or even harm.

Most black walks are improvised. While there is probably one basic walk, regional and city differences create a colorful array of walks in vogue at any given moment. The mainstay of the walk is rhythm and style. In contrast to the white male's robotlike and mechanical walk, the black walk is slower—more like a stroll. The head is slightly elevated and tipped to one side. One arm swings at the side with the hand slightly cupped. The other hand hangs straight to the side or is slipped into the pocket: "The gait is slow, casual . . . almost like a walking dance, with all parts of the body moving in rhythmic harmony."[6] Even macho sixth-grade boys can develop the swaggering, springy walk. The walk can serve as a threatening and confirming means of power in the face of hostile representatives of the mainstream: teachers, police, and store owners.

Like walking, black male stance is one of the most recognized nonverbal behaviors used to impress females during courtship rituals and to establish territory among peers. The lowered shoulder stance is the basic black position to express power and pride. With one shoulder crouched lower, the head tilted toward the shoulder, and chin protruding, the black male may then sport the stance with his hands in his pockets, tucked under the belt, or cupped loosely over the genitals. Cooke uses the term "lowered shoulder kineme" to describe this stance and says that different stances can be detected among black males: player stance, pimp stance, rapper stance, and cat stance. We see them as variations on the same theme.

Another symbolic stance is the "stationary pimp strut," in which the male puts his hands in his pockets and moves in a fluid dance to accentuate talk: "The free arm will swing, point, turn, and gesture, as conversation proceeds. It is as if they are walking in place."[7] Cooke says the "pimp stance" is used to show defiance toward authority figures.

In "peeping," the male crunches his shoulders upward and tilts one slightly higher while his head slants in the opposite direction, and his eyes take on a staring, gazing, or fixed expression. This behavior is used for courtship and calling attention to himself.

Few nonverbal behaviors symbolize the consciousness of black people and the Black Power Movement as dramatically as the black handshake. Although handwork is used to make statements of approval, solidarity, and greeting, it also signifies power, identity, and pride.

"Giving skin" and "getting skin" have many variations: palm-to-palm, agreement, complimentary, greeting, emphatic, superlative, parting, five-on-the-sly, and regular skin. Other handshakes and hand gestures used during the 1960s and 1970s were the black thumb grasp, wrist grasps, placing hands on the shoulders, flexing biceps, and making a fist. The thumb grasp is still in vogue today, but the others are less often seen. High-fives—mutual raising of arms high with palms open and touching—is popular today. Low-fives involves downward extension of the arms with palms open and touching. Both are used in sports, while high fives are often seen as everyday greetings.

African-American fraternities, gangs and other organizations have their own secret handshakes and gestures. Some fraternities use a frat shake or hand-body shake—any handwork combined with an embrace. Some call it "givin' up the da-dap." A popular black military handshake is called the "clap-hand-to-hand greeting." Variations and new inventions quickly proliferate.

Similarly, visual behavior—eye contact, gazing, staring, or rolling the eyes—gives cues to underlying feelings and intentions. Rolling the eyes conveys disapproval, anger, or dislike, especially toward authority figures. Cutting the eyes—an exaggerated moving of the eyes toward another person followed by a short stare—also expresses negative feelings. A wide repertoire of eyework is used for courting and communicating feelings and intentions between African-American males and females: Cooke calls this the "silent rap."

Research suggests that blacks look at others while listening less often than do whites.[8] Blacks make more eye contact while speaking, just the opposite of whites. In America, blacks staring at whites has often been associated with racial tension and hostility. Phil explains an encounter with a white authority figure: "Watch him, and look him in the eyes. He can't stand that! Look at him dead in his eyes and talk to him and don't take your eyes off him. You might burn your eyes, but you've psyched him out . . . that's another cool system."

Dancing

Dancing is a form of nonverbal expression that exudes freedom, creativity, spontaneity, and improvisation. The so-called "rhythmic style" in black culture is epitomized by dancing. In the 1950s and 1960s, such dances as the cool jerk and the twist were popular in the African-American community. Today, the "pop," the "cabbage patch," the "snake," and the "butt" are more likely to be seen. But no recent new dance in the 1980s gleaned as much attention from adolescents, choreographers, movie producers, advertisers, kids on the street, and even gymnasts as "breaking," or breakdancing.[9]

Breakdancing is a term that applies generically to all modern street dancing, but individual variations are myriad. Breakdancing is a fast, dizzying series of moves based on centripetal force and spinning on an axis. Most of the moves take place dangerously close to the street or floor. Sometimes flattened cardboard boxes are spread out over sidewalks to add spin. This unique art form probably was spawned in the ghettos of South Bronx as a macho street entertainment.

Forms of breakdancing include the electric boogie, the Egyptian, popping, floating, and slamdancing. Breakdancing may help prevent violence and bloodshed among young black males in the inner city. It is often used as an alternative form of fighting —a type of positive competition that expresses brotherhood and individualism at the same time.

Sports As a Vehicle for Expressiveness

Black males also use sports to express pride in themselves and their race and to show their creative style. Sports are an ideal stage for expressiveness and the cool pose. Black males have turned to sports as a way to attain competency, express masculinity, earn big money, and become famous. Sports are also a classic way to release pent-up aggression and to be powerful; these are understandably attractive motivators for historically oppressed groups, such as African-Americans.

For example, football's Butch Johnson and Billy "Whiteshoes" Johnson are two well-known black athletes who exhibit expressive behaviors on the playing field. Both are known for their fancy dances and spikes (slamming the ball to the ground in the end zone after scoring touchdowns). These two athletes, among others, also wear towels hanging from their pants, and double or triple wristbands.

Former basketball great Julius "Dr. J" Erving displayed similar expressiveness. Dr. J may have symbolized the expressive life-style better than any one sports personality. He was known for his creative, graceful athletics. Agility, flexibility, and "air hang-time" were his trademarks, in addition to his elegant moves on the court. This style of play was exemplified by his famous "ceiling climbing-high flying-gravity defying" dunks in which he was known to take off from near the foul line.

Darryl Dawkins was hailed for his extravagant showmanship on the basketball court. His "gorilla dunks" were so named because of his enormous strength. Off the court, Dawkins was famous for his verbal dexterity as a disc jockey and for his flashy clothes.

Boxers Muhammad Ali and "Sugar" Ray Leonard also epitomize the expressive life-style. Beyond their great athletic skills, these two black athletes entertain with fast hands and feet (the "Ali shuffle"), flashy showmanship, and electric personalities in and out of the ring. Ali and Leonard accentuate themselves in the ring with the display of shoe tassels (to show off magnificently speedy footwork) and the wearing of colorful robes. Ali, referred to early in his career as the "Louisville Lip," was labeled so because of his *braggadocio* and boasting, his verbal dexterity and poetry, not to mention the uncanny consistency with which he predicted the rounds in which he would knock out opponents. Ali might have been best known for his vanity, illustrated by his ritualistic hair combing after bouts. Other celebrated black athletes who epitomize the expressive life style include Connie Hawkins, famous for his fancy moves; Thomas "Hollywood" Henderson, known for his bragging and colorful personality; and Jeff Leonard, hailed for his "one flapdown homerun trot."

The expressive life-style has evolved as a way for black males to play it cool and express pride for self and race. Black males who epitomize the expressive life-style are described as cool cats. They are the subject of chapter 7.

Maybe a girl wants to go out with this guy who has a very good heart and good motives, but because of the outside influence, he's not up to date. He doesn't dress attractively, or speak eloquently. They're looking at the wrong things.

—Lou, 29

That's how girls get their feelings hurt, get taken advantage of, because they are not looking at that guy for what he is, they're looking at the outside appearance. I look at the guy on the inside. In some ways I don't care what he looks like on the outside. But if you're not taking care of yourself on the outside, I don't know . . . well, hey.

—Florrie, 23

Material coolness is not exclusive to the black community. It's everywhere.

—Charles, 27

Cool represents something bad, in some sense. I've met a lot of guys who say, oh yeah, this is being cool, I've got five girls, so what.

—Sue, 26

The negative one is very dominant. The cool guys get the freshest girls. The cool girls. Most girls want to be attractive.

—Charles, 27

The Cool Cat Life-Style

*The cat seeks through a harmonious combination of charm ... the
proper dedication to his "kick" and unrestrained generosity to make of
his day to day life itself a gracious work of art.*[1]

For many African-American males, the character that best exemplifies the expressive life-style is the cool cat. Like other forms of cool pose, being a cool cat provides a way to accentuate the self. The cool cat is an exceptional artist of expressiveness and flamboyant style. He creates his unique identity by artfully dipping into a colorful palette of clothes and hairstyles that set him apart from the ordinary. His nonverbal gestures—his walk and handshakes, for example—are mixed with high verbal agility. He can be found "rapping it down to a woman" with a flair and virtuosity that others envy. He does not simply drive a car—he "leans" (drives with one arm) and sets his neighbors talking about his self-assured risk-taking. The cool cat is the consummate actor. His performance may also be characterized by deftly manipulative and deceptive strategies.

Black males put great emphasis on style and acting cool. Appearing suave, urbane, and charming is at the heart of being a cool cat. The black male is supremely skilled at utilizing cultural symbols in a way that stamps his personal mark on all encounters. This allows him to elevate his sense of pride and control. He can broadcast strength and masculinity or shore up flagging status and dignity.

Portrait of the Cool Cat

The portrait of a typical cool cat is usually that of a young black male found on the streets of American cities. He is probably unem-

ployed, may be involved in drugs or alcohol, and has limited education. He is involved in some kind of hustling activity and is probably
from a low-income, beleaguered family. Some embrace values of
education and work and are marked by self-assurance. For example, in *Strategic Styles*, Mancini describes Hank as a "together guy"
who exudes confidence and autonomy, as well as flamboyance; he
states simply, "I got my own way in everything. I don't copy nothing
from nobody."[2]

McCord and his colleagues in *Life Styles in the Black Ghetto* char-
acterize the cool cat as a young man who spends his time on street
corners, in pool halls, or in "running some type of racket." He has a
distinctive style. Firestone defines the cool cat as a man who com-
bines charm, dedication to his "kick," and unusual generosity to
make everyday life a balanced and "gracious work of art" that contributes in some way to a pleasant, aesthetic life-style. The cool cat is
unruffled, self-assured, and eminently cool in the face of emergencies.

Clothes and the Cool Cat

Few African-American males now wear the *dashikis* of the Black
Revolution, but clothes are still used to make fashion and status
statements. Clothes help the black male attract attention and enhance his self-image. After all, in a society that has kept blacks
invisible, it is not surprising that seemingly flamboyant clothes
might be worn to heighten visibility.

Clothes can also contribute to violence and fighting, even death,
among young black males. For example, some gangs use baseball
caps or colors to symbolize gang membership. Gangs have been
known to kill youths for wearing the wrong colors or clothes. They
have also fought, occasionally to death, over brand name clothes
(such as Georgio and Gucci items), basketball sneakers, or gold
chains. Black fraternities often use jackets to indicate membership
and solidarity.

To style is the ultimate way hustlers attempt to act cool. Clothes
are a portable and creative expression of styling. The interest in
colorful male plumage begins in the early teens when attention-
getting costumes earn the young cat his place on center stage. He
begins to establish his own personal signature in dress, hairstyle,
and language. To "style," "front off," "friend," "high sign," or

"funk" all mean to show off or upstage others in a highly competitive war of masculine self-presentation. A young black woman describes how she compliments the cool cats in her life: "You all dressed up and you have your apple hat on, your flairs, and your boots and you walkin' down the street lookin' at all d' people, so you goin' style wid the lookin' good. Be more less flamboyant. . . . He's decked to kill! Da's what we [young women] tell 'em."³

Getting "clean" and dressing with style is an important way to get over in the world. Some teens see the world as a constant stage—a series of personal performances. They earn street applause for being clean and having style. Folb notes that because how you dress says so much about who you are, black males often resent wearing work-related uniforms. The uniform de-styles them. Folb quotes a youth who is contemplating quitting his job as groundskeeper aide for the County of Los Angeles: "I like to get clean and stay sharp."⁴

Hudson calls the attire of the hustler flashy and flamboyant and stresses that clothing is a central part of a hustler's front. In order to make money, he must look like he already has money (somewhat akin to the Madison Avenue grey flannel suit or recent evocations for yuppies to "dress for success"). He cannot expect to "take off some fat suckers" if he looks like a "greaseball."

When a hustler starts making money, he immediately puts his wardrobe together in order to establish prestige with his audience. A monologue by well-known black recording artist Lou Rawls describes a popular young hustler on the South Side of Chicago who epitomizes the cool cat style:

> Every Friday evening about 4:30 he would be standing there because his girlfriend works at Walgreen's . . . and on Friday, the eagle flies. He was wearing the very popular silk mohair wool worsted—continental to the bone—$250 hustler's suit . . . a pair of highly shined hustler's alligator shoes . . . white on white tab collar shirt, a very thin hustler's necktie . . . a very large artificial diamond stick pin in place . . . a hustler's hairdo . . . a process . . . hustler's shades on, cigarette in hand, a very broad smile on his face . . . staring hard and elated at what he saw . . . his automobile parked at the curb . . . white on white on white. The hustlers call them hogs, the trade name is Cadillac . . . (As the hustler is standing on the corner, he sees his wife approaching with a razor in her hand, screaming at him): You no good jiving farmer . . . the rent's not paid and the baby is hungry and

needs shoes and you're out here hustling and carrying on ... (He says): Baby, you can have this car and anything you want. Just don't cut my new suit. I just got it out of the pawn shop and I've got to have my front so I can keep on making my game.[5]

Cool Wheels

Cars also underscore the significance of style and feature heavily in "making the game." Hustlers and others in the ghetto value and treasure their automobiles. The more expensive the automobile, the more valid is the hustler's claims to have made it. As the expression goes, "he is doing good in this town."

From an early age, black teens see cars as a status symbol. Many learn to pop the ignition so they can take joyrides—preparation perhaps for organized car theft later in life. Cars allow visible, conspicuous display of status—a perfect way for the cool cat to stage his performance literally throughout the community.

One stylized type of physical posturing noted by Folb is "leaning," or "low-riding," in which the driver (and sometimes the passenger) sits so low in his seat that only the top of his head is visible and his eyes peer out over the steering wheel. Low-riding is designed to draw attention to both driver and car—a performance that may be specifically directed toward females. Folb quotes a young woman's perception of these performances:

Leanin' that's when a dude be leanin' so hard like he layin' down in d' car. Da's what they do in their cars. Lean like, "I'm jus' the man. But guys in low-ridin' cars lean and low ride 'cause they know they gotta be funky and they say, "Well, the car be lookin' good, I gotta look good."[6]

For the cool cat, driving a Cadillac (or other luxury car) is important for more than just transportation. Cadillac-type cars epitomize class because of their reputation and because they take up a great deal of physical space. They symbolize being seen—a critical experience for those who have been invisible in this country for so long. The cool cat feels, "If I can drive a stylish car like this, it proves to myself and others that I am as important as anyone else. I haven't given up. I am going to make it." The cool cat often sacrifices other economic goods in his life or his family's life to have a big luxury car as a way to make such a statement.

Lame to the Bone

If style is the ultimate way to act cool, cool cats must have definite beliefs as to what represents nonstylistic behavior. Being called "lame to the bone" or "uncool" is the ultimate insult in black teenage vernacular. Being lame means to be socially incompetent, disabled, or crippled—a sissy. The "lame brand" does not even know how to talk to females; he may appear frightened of them. Folb reports:

> Dudes be talkin' to d' young lady, he run aroun', shootin' marbles. Not too situated . . . Dumb sucker have no girls, don't know where everything is . . . stone SUCKER! Sissy boy, hangin' 'round his momma all the time. Dedicated to d' home front. He don't know what's happ'nin'. He like a school book chump . . . stupid, ignorant, hide in d' books all d' time—like a bookworm. He square to d' wood! . . . Don't get high, don't smoke no weed. Show 'im a reefer, he wouldn't even know what it is! . . . Uncoordinated. He cain't fight or nothin'. Like he followin' you everplace you go . . . wanna be wid everybody but don't do nothin' . . . They can't catch on to what's happ'nin'.[7]

For those who are lame, there is probably no hope of rehabilitation.

Half-stepping means to do something halfway and is a form of being lame or uncool. A person who is not appropriately dressed for an occasion is not mounting the correct performance. If he is giving a party, he should not dress the way he would for school or work, in off-brand tennis shoes or Levis, or wrinkled clothing: "Don't come half-steppin', come fiendish, righteously dap to a tee, silk to the bone. Or like a date. Like you dress yo'self up—some bad-boy bell bottom, nice shirt. Don't half step. Get yo'self together brother."[8]

Why Is Style So Important?

We might ask why style is so important to cool cats. Styling helps cool cats draw attention to the self and communicates creativity.

The African-American man in this country has been "nobody" for generations. The purpose of styling, then, is to paint a self-portrait in colorful, vivid strokes that makes the black male "somebody."

The extravagant, flashy clothes often worn by cool cats, the blaring ghettoblasters playing earsplitting music as they walk or drive down the street, signify their need to be seen and heard. Styling is an antidote to invisibility and silence, a hope in a hopeless world, a defense against multiple attacks on cultural and personal integrity. It is proactive rather than defensive. Styling lets the black male show others that he is alive, and reminds himself as well.

The cool cat styles for the cosmetic effect (how he looks) and to symbolize the messages he wants to portray: "No matter how poor I am or what has happened to me in the past, this shows that I can still make it . . . and with class."

Irrespective of race or class, it is not enough to survive or just live from day to day in a social vacuum. Rather, individuals have a genuine need to know that they can make a contribution to their own welfare and personal growth and that they have control over their own destiny. That they can be noticed and can better their lives.

Perkins writes that black children internalize the roles that will allow them to perform on the only stage they know: the black ghetto colony. The cool cat and similar roles are adopted because they have great survival value, not just because they elicit applause from the immediate audience. Black children learn how to be cool under the most extenuating circumstances because being cool is a clear advantage. Perkins adds that when a situation is fraught with danger or anxiety (becomes "uptight"), the most sophisticated response is being cool, "hip," or "together." Cool stabilizes the situation and either minimizes or ignores threats that cannot be easily dealt with in other ways.

Firestone sees the "idea cat" as a person who is adequate to any situation. He adopts a cool image in order to deal with status and identity problems in a society that denies equal access. Foster hypothesizes that as the black man's drive for middle-class status in the North was thwarted by racism, a cool street-corner lifestyle evolved. White racism in urban areas both stimulates and perpetuates street-corner behavior. Whereas other ethnic groups have been allowed to assimilate after a period of initial bigotry, doors have remained impermeable to African-Americans. (Foster notes that where the doors have been opened for black males, a highly organized street life-style is not as likely to develop.) In most places in America, those doors remain at least partially closed.

The cool cat life-style has long functioned as a means to enhance the black male's ability to survive the harsh effects of racism and social oppression. Because of a lack of resources, services, goods, information, and jobs, lower-income blacks often have hours of free time on their hands. The cool cat life-style provides a kind of stimulation and entertainment. Something is always going on or being contemplated. Those who live in the ghetto often view cool cats as fashionable, hip, cool, and chic. This glamorized life-style helps the black male to achieve balance—entertainment and stimulation counter frustration and boredom.

Being a cool cat is one route toward creative masculinity, toward recognition. It helps black males to survive, to style and act cool, to show disdain for the white man and the Protestant work ethic, and to show pride and dignity. It enhances manhood, commands respect, vents bitterness and anger, establishes a sense of control, expresses artistry, accentuates the self, and provides a form of amusement.

Life on the Streets

For cool cats who like to style, the streets are the best place to hustle and earn a living. The streets are exhilarating, perilous, electric with possibilities, and lush with social meaning. As with some other groups, such as Hispanics, the streets are the main stage of daily life for black males. For whites and for middle-class blacks, the streets are just concrete pathways of neutrality and practicality, perhaps even of danger. For young blacks, especially those who live in impoverished inner-city neighborhoods, the streets become the community living room, the sports arena, the recreation hall, the marketplace, and the political forum. Drug deals, hanging out, love affairs, gang rivalries, and training in conventional wisdom all take place in the streets.

The streets are a school for life that easily competes with the dry, often irrelevant pap squeezed between pages of books in nearby school buildings. H. Rap Brown remembers his own early years in the ghetto. He says the streets are where "young bloods" seek and gain control and where they receive their most relevant education: "I learned how to talk in the streets, not from reading about Dick and Jane going to the zoo and all that simple shit. Sometimes I wonder why I ever bothered to go to school. Practically everything I know I learned on the corner."[9]

Phil talks about how the streets are his home and the place he learned to keep his true feelings to himself: "I am a street person. A street person will not tell The Man everything. Like you can't be too honest, man. Go ahead and be honest, you goin' wish you had not. You don't tell the truth all the time. You're screwing yourself up! I learned that shit from the white man."

Streets are where it happens—it being whatever holds emotional valence for the young black male. Streets are beyond parental control. Streets respond to the authority of youth and gangs, rather than of age, parents, teachers, or police. The streets train for criminality, not conventionality. For many, the streets become home for most of the day and night. Home (meaning house) becomes a place to catch a few hours of sleep and to dress for the next main stage (street) performance. For others, the streets become home, literally—or their coffin.

A young black boy raised by a prostitute mother and an alcoholic father remembers when he began to develop the street-smart ways of a cool cat, liking the taste of cheap liquor, and meeting all the neighborhood's cats—the gamblers, pimps, bootleggers, and hustlers:

> I knew the ministers, teachers, and deacons of the church who came to the districts to do no preaching or teaching. I knew the city and county officials who, in secret, slipped me quarters whenever they came for their share of the "dirty money" or just seeking the favor of the ladies . . . I remember the sharp gamblers who spent their spare time hanging around with my beautiful mother. They played with me and taught me the tricks of the trade. At nine, I knew how to ink and crimp the other guy's cards between my fingers. I remember the flashy clothes of the gamblers and pimps and sharp automobiles.[10]

The young boy's early training in such illegal activities as pimping, gambling, bootlegging, and prostitution prepared him for the fast life. He wanted to grow up to be just like these role models, reflecting the urgency of black males in the ghetto who are exposed to alternative life-styles and roles during their tenderest years. If they learn their lessons well, they can survive later as cool hustlers.

Hustling to Fill the Void

The cool cat life-style is a survival strategy par excellence because this role develops as a reaction to racism and social oppression. The art of hustling, expressed in various forms of deceptive and manipulative activities, is the cool cat's greatest weapon against poverty and social inequality. Hustling becomes the African-American male's original and indigenous means of waging a private war on poverty. Some believe that hustling is a more successful antipoverty weapon than the government has invented to date.

Foster writes that hustling, as a profession, is a way of life for many black men. It requires only a "degree from the streets." Horton asked some black males, "When a dude needs bread (money), how does he get it?" The universal response was "the hustle." Hustling, as the primary street activity, becomes the economic foundation for everyday life and sets the tone of social activities as well.

Hustling for the cool cat represents not only an alternative economic form, but an alternative form of masculinity. Black males have accepted the basic masculine goals, norms, and standards of our society (such as wanting to work and provide for a family), but unlike white males, they lack the means to achieve these masculine goals. Resolute attempts to work hard in legitimate jobs are, for many black males, met with being the last hired and first fired, low pay, insult, or lack of promotion. Playing the American game according to the standard rules does not necessarily lead to upward social or occupational mobility.

The constant pressure to prove his manhood without mainstream tools has left many black males feeling angry and bitter. They feel they have been locked out of the American mainstream. The cool cat life-style is a way to mock whites and the Protestant work ethic by exploiting, rapping, conning, the "pimping game," and other hustling roles.

Hustling roles say to the white man: "Hustling makes me feel like a man and allows me to survive. But more important, I hustle, white man, because it is something you hate, and it therefore defies the principles you are most proud of . . . the Protestant work ethic. And even though I realize this life-style can potentially destroy me, at least I make a strong statement to you, white man, that no matter what happens by this hustling, I was in control, not you, and this is all that matters."

Hustling compensates for lack of income, goods and services, and status. It gives the cool cat a kit bag of identity tools for creating a sense of power, prestige, pride, and manhood. The road to mainstream American success is opened, at least for the moment or for the day. The oppressed man can use cool and hustling as his best chance to advance financially and socially and to feel important.

Foster believes that considerable talent is expended in pulling off the street-corner hustle. If racism and exploitation by whites had not pulled the plug on legitimate means for establishing masculinity, illegal outlets would not have thrived. He argues that countless young black males—cool cats and hustlers supreme—who have shown talent in their pursuit of the illegitimate game, would have shown extreme giftedness in the pursuit of mainstream avenues to success.

The street corner hustlers might have become aggressive salesmen, businessmen, or politicians under more favorable conditions. But in the face of restricted opportunities, lack of middle-class black role models, and confronted with the successful models of the hustler and pimp, the young black male is tempted to take the street route to success. Ironically, the street man and the mainstream man both want the same thing. Both want to make it and to be seen by their families and friends as secure and successful—as somebody. But each sees a different road as the logical one to take.

Hudson offers an intriguing idea: although hustling might appear to be diametrically opposed to the Protestant ethic, it is actually an extension of it. He hypothesizes that the hustler's society may be deviant, but it is an adaptive, systematic form of deviance that struggles toward mainstream rewards and goals.

Survival dictates the cool cat's course. He accepts the expressive, cool path of the street because he quickly or eventually comes to believe that conventional routes are congested or closed off to him. For the cool cat who travels the road of hustling, conning, and gaming, pitfalls, as well as fame, may be around the corner.

The manner he approaches that girl is totally different from the way he really feels. We know he's cool, but he's "acting" himself. Maybe she doesn't understand.

—Gina, 22

The way we think of coolness, there's no specific way that a cool person would relate to women. It's individualistic, it's what his motives and his interests are with the opposite sex. That's another thing on being cool . . . to have girls.

—Bob, 17

Sex is what they want. They don't go back to the traditions. Nowadays, a guy, like, "yo baby, I want to take you out." Instead of wanting to go and meet your family, they want to take you out, then dump you after they did what they did. I've been through that before. You don't wanna see my family, you don't wanna see me. They're really low.

—Mavis, 27

Some of the guys have a big chip on their head. It's hard to find a guy who's got a nice job. Guys say, I'm number one, and if you don't like me, then . . .

—Sue, 26

Girls are not everything in the world. Anybody can do girls, but it depends on what that girl is all about. Is she all about what you've got in your pocket, or what you've got in your heart?

—Mavis, 27

8

Playing the Dozens

We played the dozens for recreation, like white folks play Scrabble.
—H. Rap Brown

Playing the dozens exemplifies the expressive life-style, especially for young African-American males. It represents a way to act and be cool with astonishingly intricate verbal play. Playing the dozens helps adolescent black males maintain control and keep cool under adverse conditions. It prepares them for the socioeconomic problems they may later face and facilitates their search for masculinity, pride, status, social competence, and expressive sexuality.

This highly stylized verbal repartee, which to some extent serves as a safety valve for ambivalent feelings toward women, is also a form of entertainment and stimulation. The dozens is a unique cultural phenomenon that has developed in many African-American communities; it is a game that cuts across social class boundaries, but is more likely to be found in low-income areas. A ritualized verbal contest, it is also known as "momma talky," sounding, joning, woofing, sigging, or signifying. Adolescent black males are the prime players, but some black females and white teens also engage in this verbal display.

African-American culture has often been referred to as an oral culture, one rich with storytelling and verbal repartee. The power of words to comfort, elevate status, defend, sexually arouse, and convince is well-respected. Adherence to masculinity and toughness is often displayed through ritualistic storytelling and accounts of successfully managing conflict or tight situations. Oliver notes that stories are highlighted by claims of what was said to the antagonist and how verbal threats were used to handle challenges to self-image or physical well-being. Playing the dozens is a ritualized form of this long-standing verbal tradition.

The common language that has developed to ensure survival helps blacks articulate shared pain, sorrow, humor, and joy. As a distinctive mode of expression, it serves to wall off oppression and build solidarity within the community. The dozens is simply an extreme utterance of this private language.

Grier and Cobbs, in *The Jesus Bag*, hold that, "In the miracle that is culture, the dozens may be a highly evolved instrument of survival by means of which black boys are introduced to the humiliations which will become so intimate a part of their life."[1] But in the context of the game, these humiliations are squeezed into rhyming couplets that testify to the player's ability to keep cool under mounting pressure.

The Insult War

The dozens is a verbal contest that plays a significant role in the psychological and linguistic development of young blacks. It may also reflect the high verbal ability of some youths who enjoy the trial of a verbal war that is shunned by mainstream culture, yet subculturally esteemed. The game reflects the uniquely expressive nature of black talk with its special rhythms, inflections, slangs, and grammar. Abrahams describes the dozens as two protagonists hurling insults against each other and their families. The audience spurs on the exchange with words of encouragement or ridicule. Each must defend his honor and that of his family in a new stream of insulting epithets against which, in turn, his opponent must respond just as eloquently. The contest ends when people lose interest, a physical fight erupts (which is rare), or a third party intervenes.

McCormick describes the dozens as a game "in which the players strive to bury one another with vituperation." Mothers are subject to vicious slander; fathers are "queer, syphilitic"; "sisters are whores, brothers are defective, cousins are 'funny' and the opponent is himself diseased."[2] Accusations of cowardice, homosexuality, or stupidity are common.

Similarly, Dove writes that the dozens is a contest to see which brother can devise the greatest number of rhymed couplets to destroy the reputation of the opponent or his parents. Young males try to outstrip each other insult against insult in a sometimes vicious, sometimes obscene, war of words. They deprecate each other's family in a black tradition of one-upmanship in which women, especially mothers, are often the prime targets. Gestures, body stances, and tonality accompany clever repartee that makes its point at the expense of someone close to the contestants.

Ritualized Sexuality

Berdie, an early observer of the dozens in the 1940s, defines the game as a formalized expression of verbal aggression in which opponents try to bring each other to the point of initiating physical combat. As the exchange becomes progressively nasty and pornographic, virtually every family member and every sexual act is woven into the verbal assault. These rhymes are examples of the dozens:

I.
I fucked your mama
Till she went blind
Her breath smells bad,
But she sure can grind
I fucked your mama
For a solid hour
Screaming, Black Power.
Elephant and the Baboon
Learning to screw.
Baby came out looking
Like Spiro Agnew.[3]

II.
I was walking through the jungle
With my dick in my hand
I was the baddest mother-fucker in
The jungle land.
I looked up in the tree
And what did I see?
Your little black mama
Trying to piss on me.
I picked up a rock
And hit her in the cock

> And knocked that bitch
> A half a block
> I hate to talk about your mama
> She's a sweet old soul
> She got a rap-pa-tap-pa tap dick
> And a pussy hole.
> Listen mother fucker
> You a two-timing bitch
> You got a ring around your pussy
> Make an old man rich.[4]

As illustrated by these two examples, the dozens game emphasizes sexual and pornographic material. Schulz observes that the dozens acquaints both males and females with sexuality at an early age, often before they would otherwise learn about it.

As a sexual primer, Hannerz believes that the dozens and other "obscene songs" of black inner-city males help free them from dependency on mother figures. At the same time, playing the dozens educates them toward female sexuality. Those who play the dozens are pubescent and adolescent males; their preoccupation with sex is not surprising.

Because early adolescence is a period of both cognitive and physiological maturation, it would seem logical for these young black males to emphasize sexual matters in the dozens game as a way to test and release sexual energy as they begin to mature physically.

As we mentioned in chapter 7, African-Americans seem to be exposed to more diverse sexual experiences much earlier in their lives than members of typical white families. Because of this, blacks are likely to be more open, sensitive, and comfortable with sexual matters when compared to whites. The dozens game, then, may act as a natural extension and acceptance of this cultural attitude and may give the dozens its sexual twist. Young black males may use the dozens game to show off their hip or cool attitude toward sex. They may also use the game to test out, make fun of, or embarrass individuals from families with limited exposure to sexual matters. For those males whose families are less open about discussing sex, the dozens game may provide initial exposure to the forbidden fruit that adolescents everywhere find so fascinating.

Black adolescent females may help to shape and socialize the males in their use of sexually related material in the dozens game, possibly because of their similar interests or stage of development or because of the entertainment the dozens game offers them.

Rhyming and Expressiveness

Rhyming is an important part of the dozens game. More importantly, rhyming may cover up sexual and pornographic material to make it more acceptable to adults. Expressing antisocial sentiments and engaging in verbal obscenities is risky business. The rhyming may reduce that risk by veiling and confounding meanings, although much of the content of the dozens is explicitly obscene. Rhyming also seems to have a natural affinity with the expressive life-style.

Rhyming may act as a mnemonic aid to enhance learning the dozens. Studies have shown that children learn how to spell, comprehend, and memorize subject matter in school much faster when it is combined with music to help stimulate right-brain processes. Similarly, rhyming may act to help young black males to learn, comprehend, and memorize the dozens game more efficiently.

Ambivalence toward Women

Even though the dozens game is a form of entertainment, it stimulates ambivalence among young black males because pornographic material, directed at a mother, often causes guilt, confusion, and altercations: One insult toward a mother is enough to start the competition.

Because racism and social oppression often prevent African-American males from being able to provide for their families, many lower-income black families are father-absent. Young males are often brought closer to the needs and feelings of their mothers because of their fathers' absence and inability to provide for the family. Because the youth is constantly exposed to the problems and sacrifices of his mother's attempt to raise a family without a co-provider, he may become unexpectedly sensitive, protective, and empathetic toward his mother and other women. He may take on more responsibilities and mature faster when compared to other adolescent groups.

This empathetic attitude many black adolescent males have toward their mothers contributes to their ambivalence toward the dozens game. The love-hate feeling toward the game may be a result of two competing values: the positive rewards of entertainment and psychosocial development versus the negative rewards of pornographic insults directed at one's mother. Black males often play the dozens with mixed feelings and frequently forbid any kind of insults or name-calling directed at a mother. Fights are not unusual for players who attempt to take the game past prescribed limits. It is likely that the dozens evolved as a game to focus on mothers because of strong feelings of love, respect, empathy, and sensitivity; the reactions the game might invoke when pornographic material is directed at one's mother are likely to be equally powerful.

For the black adolescent male, the dozens game might be defined as a rite of passage because of the way it tests his control, character, and courage. In the final analysis, if he can handle the insults peers direct at his mother in the dozens, then it is likely he can take whatever insults society might hurl at him.

Ribbing: Zeroing In on Personal Defects

As well as exploiting women, the dozens game also uses information that highlights the contestants' personal deficiencies. Black adolescent males have become aware of their own personal and social limitations. It is tempting to speculate that they have developed keener perceptual skills and cues, as compared to other adolescent groups, as a way to enhance their chances of self-preservation. In focusing on the personal deficiencies of others, the dozens game may help to take the attention off their own deficiencies. Using the dozens game as an offensive weapon may represent a well-established defense.

Parker observes that blacks learn early in life how to analyze and attack basic beliefs held by others. The person being attacked also learns very early how to defend himself through a process called "ribbing." Ribbing can target what the opponent is wearing and how he walks, talks, or relates to others.

The Crowd As Catalyst

Historically, the game of dozens was played, for the purpose of amusement, in front of a small crowd of peers. As a collective game that invites audience participation, the dozens still often takes place before a group.

Dollard sees the crowd as essential to the game. The gathering crowd serves to magnify insults and demand repartee. It acts as an amplifier and catalyst for upping the ante of progressively audacious insults. Eager for a battle, the crowd eggs participants on. The fear of ridicule may seduce antagonists into a fight, even when they might prefer to drop the matter. The audience spurs the contestants on with increasingly disparaging insults, which keeps the game exciting. The crowd rewards witty, cutting remarks with cheers but scorns weak rejoinders. The players rev up to a brilliantly intense exchange, trying to make each rhyme funnier, filthier, or more caustic than the last.

Abrahams believes that losing the dozens in front of the crowd can be devastating. The loser may be seen as ineffectual, or even worse, effeminate.

A Cruel but Skillful Game

In many ways, then, the dozens is a cruel game. Words are weapons aimed at destruction of another man's honor and pride. The stakes of this battle are high. Fighting with words replaces physical fights that could lead to injury or death. Humiliation and anger rise to a feverish pitch as the taunting proceeds to draw the other into a fight, or reduce him to tears. H. Rap Brown recalls:

> You'd say shit like, "Man, tell your mama to stop coming around my house all the time. I'm tired of fucking her and I think you should know it ain't no accident you look like me." . . . It was a bad score for the dude that was getting humiliated. I seldom was. That's why they call me Rap, 'cause I could rap.[5]

Those who could not rap were doubly humiliated: first for being born black, and then for losing in front of their own people.

Origins of the Dozens

The dozens game rests on high verbal expressiveness and social competence—two qualities that are key to black survival. As Abrahams explains, one of the values of the African-American community that differentiates it from white culture is the high status given to the adept verbal performer. The young performer epitomizes black culture. The talker as performer is "on" all the time. Verbal behavior is judged as a performance, and the speaker is judged as if he were onstage. Any conversation can turn into a dramatic scene at any time.

Speculation about the origins of the dozens leads us back to the slavery period, as is true for so many of the unique black social processes we are discussing in this book. One theory is that, like black masking and black humor, the dozens originated with American field slaves who used the game in place of physical assault on untouchable, higher-status house slaves. Field slaves would be lashed or deprived of food if they harmed the often pampered house servants. Cotton pickers, sugarcane workers, and other field laborers suffered from the shame of lower status and poorer conditions as compared to such generally lighter-skinned house workers as butlers, coachmen, lackeys, maids, and housekeepers. The uniforms of the house slaves bespoke a privileged status in a pitiful pecking order based on skin color, and sometimes on chance. Field slaves could vent their spleen by insulting their parents and remote ancestors. If the insults worked and the house slaves showed discomfort, the vilification became even more lewd and vulgar. The name "dozens" may have derived from the notion that the opponent's mother was supposed to be one of the dozens of women available to the sexual whims of her master.

Levine supports the argument that the dozens game serves as a way to keep things cool. From slavery onward, being able to "take it has been highly virtuous and often essential. The example of Jesus may have served as an inspiration, as a slave relates: 'They crucified my lord, an' He never said a mumblin' word.' "[6]

Holding feelings in under incredible stress is a discipline fostered by the ritualistic insults in the dozens game, which was, we think, developed under slavery—a time when African-Americans were the butt of insidious insults on their dignity. Keeping cool then was the only safe response; keeping cool now is still the only safe response.

In addition, oral tradition is generally pervasive in black culture. Fast talking had great survival value during the slavery period and continues to confer prestige and promote survival up to the present day. Verbal dexterity is highly valued in the black community: Youngsters play verbal games with each other as a pleasurable pastime. Talking almost becomes an instrument that children learn to play early in life. Folb says that the banter, taunting, and pleasure of playing with words helps black children develop vocabulary and earns them a place in their peer groups.

Ability with words is as highly valued as physical strength. Dealing with The Man is less likely to result in incarceration or beatings if one uses verbal rather than physical force. This high verbal skill developed by some black youths is not rewarded in schools that demand silence and stress written rather than oral abilities. For this reason, the same verbal agility that brings black youths status on the streets often gets them into trouble in school.

According to LaFever, one way to be socially rewarded and attain high status in the black community is to develop exceptional language ability, which then becomes the foundation for ritualized behavior such as playing the dozens. Hammond concurs: Being able to "talk that talk" brings prestige and the esteem of his peers. Boykins argues further that talking is performance, not merely a vehicle for interacting or communicating. For black adolescents, then, playing the dozens is a performance because of the expressive, verbal skills necessary to the game. It is also a measure of social or interpersonal competence.

This verbal "aesthetic of the cool," as Hammond calls it, is a vehicle for asserting control and gaining attention in a world that offers black males few other routes to competence. The game often imitates adult hip expressiveness, either in language or in body talk. Sometimes older brothers serve as instructors and informal audiences for extemporaneous practice sessions.

Why is verbal ability such a highly regarded skill in the African-American community? One reason is that it often makes the difference between getting by and getting ahead. Many role models for black youth—pimps, entertainers, musicians, ministers, and politicians—make it because of their fancy mouthwork. Those who can emulate them can become miniheroes themselves. Abrahams and Gay say that verbal ability "can make the difference between having or not having food to eat, a place to live, clothes to wear, being accepted or rejected by one's peers, and being personally and emotionally secure or risking a complete loss of ego."[7]

Filling the Void: Play and Entertainment

Black males who live in the ghetto have had to create their own forms of entertainment to keep from being bored and living life in a social vacuum. Playing the dozens provides the kind of stimulation and entertainment that is so often lacking in inner-city neighborhoods. Young men play the dozens at least in part to have fun and kill time. Kochman adds that playing the dozens energizes young males and relieves the boredom that tends to fill a restrictive environment.

Huizinga, in *Homo Ludens*, makes reference to several general characteristics of play relative to culture. While Huizinga's study deals with play generically, his analysis can be applied to the dozens. The dozens, as a form of ritualized play and entertainment, shares many of Huizinga's characteristics of play. For example, play creates order in an otherwise imperfect, confused world. It results in the development of a "play-community" that shares something important and withdraws, albeit temporarily, from the rest of the world. This creates a feeling of belonging among players, a feeling of being "apart-together." If the play uses secret rules or language, as in the dozens, the feeling that the activities are for "us," not for "others" is enhanced. Play also defines rules for inside the circle that may differ radically from the customs of everyday life. The usual rules for social interaction may not count in play.

Establishing a Rep

The accent on verbal performance and competence in the dozens game also has psychosocial implications relating to the development of the adolescent black male's "rep," or reputation. His status, identity, and masculinity ride on his reputation as a cool, competent player. In the concrete anonymity of inner-city streets, he must find ways to dramatize himself. Verbal performances showcased in the dozens are one way to take center stage. Being able to joke, engage in verbal games, and "talk shit" adds to his reputation.

The young male who raps or plays the dozens with masterful flair epitomizes the black street life-style. The centrality of this skill is reflected in the writings of Malcolm X and H. Rap Brown, who both acknowledge how important it was for them to learn to "talk right" and to establish their reps through talk wherever they went.

The man who is poor in money, jobs, services, or resources can be rich in reputation based on his verbal agility.

Keeping Cool with the Dozens

The most important contribution of the dozens game may be as a coping mechanism to help teach black adolescent males how to control their feelings. Learning how to keep cool, monitor tempers, anger, frustration, pent-up aggression, and other anxieties is crucial in the black world.

Ossie Guffy in her book, *Ossie: The Autobiography of a Black Woman*, uses an anecdote to highlight the importance of the dozens game as a mechanism for self-control. She begins the story by describing how she and four other youngsters were playing on her grandfather's farm. One boy was hit and instead of hitting back started insulting the others with the dozens. Overhearing this, her grandfather lectured and paddled them:

> "When I was coming up," Grandpa said, "I heard about that game, only I heard about it the way it used to be, and I heard how it started and why it started. It was a game slaves used to play, only they wasn't just playing for fun. They was playing to teach themselves and their sons how to stay alive. The whole idea was to learn to take whatever the master said to you without answering back or hitting him 'cause that was the way a slave had to be, so's he could go on living. It maybe was a bad game, but it was necessary. It ain't necessary now."[8]

Once Ossie's mother had found out what had happened, she pointed out that although the boys should not have been using bad words, the game would teach them how to hold their tempers in check.

The severely restrictive rituals of this game help young boys play out, in a highly controlled fashion, otherwise overpowering feelings of rage, hostility, and frustration. White also believes that the dozens helps blacks keep cool and think fast under pressure, without revealing their true feelings. The dozens is a nonviolent way to deal with potentially violent feelings inspired by society, community, peers, and family. It is a protective device designed to avoid victimization. Physical reactions or verbalizing feelings directly might be socially, economically, or even physically suicidal.

Playing the dozens helps the black male raise his threshold of tolerance for frustration. In an ironic twist on the old saw, "sticks and stones may break my bones, but names will never hurt me," the dozens brings the art of verbal assault to the place where it is in fact as painful as physical assault. But if he can learn to weather this attack on his dignity and remain cool, in control, and able to retaliate in kind, the black male can weather anything.

Playing the dozens ("woofing" or "sounding") is a way for the young black male to defend attacks on his manhood. By verbally attacking and gaming, rather than resorting to physical violence, he can defend his identity. Black males who engage in these verbal contests regard them as entertainment and as an alternative to violence. As Kochman argues, the purpose is to gain a sense of respect and fear from others without becoming violent. This requires creating an aura of being fearless and tough. It is a symbolic act that is designed to advertise one's willingness to become involved in violence if the verbal contest fails.

With playing the dozens, we close our detailed portrayal of the various areas that comprise cool pose. In chapter 9, we explore implications of cool behavior for intervention and further research.

I don't think this behavior will change. It's actually advancing; you see the negative side more and more every day. I don't see an immediate change in the pressure pushing blacks to be cool negatively. In fact it's increasing every day. It's becoming a dilemma in the black society. It hurts to see that there's no improvement in that area.

—Chuck, 33

I think there will be change with the different programs with the community really helping these young kids that are strung out on drugs, these young girls that are getting pregnant. But they have to be motivated, and we as a community have to be motivated to help them.

—John, 38

Cool should be something that comes from his heart: his principles, conduct, his way of life. Taking things as they are and finding the best way to handle situations when they arise.

—Sonny, 17

9

Summary and Implications

*An American Negro isn't a man
—he's a walking defense mechanism.*
—Frank Yerby

But can a people live and develop . . . [by] simply reacting?
—Ralph Ellison

We have described cool pose as a mechanism used by some black males to cope with the realities of their existence. The purpose of posing and posturing—being cool—is to enhance social competence, pride, dignity, self-esteem, and respect. Cool enhances masculinity. Being cool also expresses bitterness, anger, and distrust toward the dominant society for many years of hostile mistreatment and discrimination. Cool pose helps keep the dominant society off balance and puzzled and accentuates the expressive self. It is in this context that we define cool pose as a creative strategy devised by African-American males to counter the negative forces in their lives.

We have shown the historical, social, and cultural significance of cool in the lives of black males and have outlined the dilemmas facing them as we move toward the year 2000. In this final chapter, we first discuss the negative bias present in research on blacks and suggest some ways to construct more positive models. In the second section, we suggest some social programs, interventions, and policy changes that might improve the conditions under which black males in America live.

Toward a Positive Model of Black Masculinity

Black males in this country have been outstanding husbands, fathers, boyfriends, and men in many different ways. But historically, social science literature has tended to view black males negatively. Analysis of the social condition of black males in America all too often proceeds from a deficit model. As Young points out, most studies tend to approach the status of African-Americans from a pathological or social problems perspective.

Robinson, Bailey, and Smith claim that black males are portrayed negatively. They are defined as a problem the African-American family must endure, rather than as a functional, contributing family member. Even when the low-income urban black family is intact (contains both male and female partners), the suspicion remains that the husband/father may not be around for long. He is seen as a temporary actor, an interloper, or an anomaly.

With few exceptions, social scientists have tended to ignore middle-income, educated, and successful black males. They have tended to neglect father-present families and to ignore the positive aspects of a male's presence, even when he is not living in the household. When father absence is a variable in studies, the presence of another stable, committed male is often overlooked, thus confounding research results. Studies that concentrate on situations in which black men are only minimally involved in family affairs overshadow those in which black men have dedicated themselves to their wives and children. A few studies feature economically secure black men who dominate familial authority and provide well for their families. And only a very few explore the lives of African-American men who live complex, middle-class, or professional lives with extended involvement in family, community, and national arenas.

In fact, however, many black families benefit from the presence of committed fathers, husbands, and companions. The black family, frequently matriarchal, low-income, and welfare-dependent, would be even worse off if men had not been contributing all along. And many black families are headed by strong, committed, hard-working men—patriarchs who have the respect of their children, partners, and communities.

Most Are Not Murderers

The negative bias in social science is mirrored in literature and the media, which of course reflect general perceptions of black men. Black actress and activist Ruby Dee, aware of these negative impressions, illustrates the problem:

> . . .one night I was watching the news on T.V. and hoping that the killer being talked about wouldn't turn out to be a black man and I found my inside-self jumping up and shouting, Hold on! Most black men aren't murderers, thieves, aren't in jail, haven't deserted their families. Most black men don't live lives that reaffirm all the negatives they've been taught to suspect about themselves . . . [1]

She goes on to recall the concerned black men of Philadelphia who, every year, single out black youths for awards and scholarships. She admits that there are many black males for whom the inherited hurts of slavery and racism create more pressure than they can bear but cautions that black male consciousness has been pounded with suspicions of wrongdoing, even when they are doing right.

Most black men make the headlines only when they commit a crime, fail in their quest for success and survival, or fall prey to substance abuse. Those who are supportive of their families, who are attentive to their children, who offer love, understanding, and encouragement to "women who couldn't have progressed in their chosen work" without it, or who are politicians, teachers, musicians, doctors, lawyers, businessmen, and ordinary workers, also deserve headlines. Dee believes that black men who served in the military during Vietnam and other wars have not been appropriately recognized or were recognized too late. She calls for "headlines about all those black men who overwhelm the ugly statistics and the negative assessments with their grace and style and elegance of spirit."

Susan Taylor, editor of *Essence* magazine, is aware of the negative impressions people often have of black males. She argues in an editorial entitled "Give the Man a Hand" that there is essentially a war being waged on blacks in America, and the "cannons are pointed directly at our men." Taylor writes that pain has been the central theme in the lives of black men: They have, since slavery, been whipped, shackled, and castrated, both physically and mentally. Yet black males have been able to fight back, in spite of a lack of education and negative media images. Taylor suggests that the plight of black males has affected their lives with women: "I'm not an apologist for black men. Like most sisters, I've had my share of blues with the brothers. And in retrospect it was often because they were struggling with their own lives."[2]

When she looks black men in the eye, Taylor sees the pain and confusion that emanate from chronic unemployment, insulting wages, keeping up the front, and trying to feel like men in modern America. She believes that the messages regarding manhood that are sent to black men create a deadly trap. Respect is measured in "cash or clout," both of which are extremely difficult for black men to obtain in a racist, discriminatory society:

> What kind of behavior can you expect from a young man who's gotten the message that to feel powerful he must plant his seed and wear $60 sneakers and a $500 leather suit? What kind of behavior should we expect from the youngster when he can't even get a job and we've given him no other standards by which to define his manhood?[3]

Although black men have been blocked in their pursuit of manhood, Taylor, like Dee, believes they should be given credit for achieving as much as they have. If they have become empowered, it has been against incredible odds. If equity prevailed, black men would be equally distributed throughout the upper and middle strata of economic, political, and entertainment arenas.

Taylor adds that black women who expect their men to act according to white standards (or admire the image of manhood portrayed on TV, in the movies, and in romance novels) should rethink their vision of love and how they respond to black men. Like the black woman's experience in America, the black man's journey "ain't been no crystal stair either." For both, the wounds of marginalization and rejection run deep.

That black women are beginning to advocate for their male counterparts is yet another sign that survival depends on empathy, the destruction of negative stereotypes, positive approaches to understanding, and every effort to put aside our tendency to blame the victim.

Broaden the Research Agenda

Unfortunately, many black males will continue to engage in compulsive masculinity and the negative aspects of cool pose as long as there is oppression and a perception of racism. The consequences will continue to plague our society and the black community unless we begin to consider other ways of viewing this phenomenon. Social scientists and public policy analysts must begin to engage in scholarship that focuses not only on how structural pressures contribute to violence among black males—although that is surely a critical question—but also on the subjective cultural reality of black male life and interpersonal styles.

Scholars and analysts must try to analyze how cultural processes shape and affect values, attitudes, and actions. Anything short of a combined structural and cultural analysis of the black male experience will serve only to maintain the mysterious and enigmatic image of the black male and will perpetuate current problems.

Further study of cool pose as an important reflection of subjective cultural realities for black males should be addressed within the context of definitions of masculinity. Unfortunately, most of the research to date has been influenced by Moynihan's concept of the pathological and antisocial nature of the black matriarchal family, the impact of father absence, and the ostensibly negative effects of such family patterns on the ego development of black males.

Instead, we need much more research on how race, class, gender, and socioeconomic forces help to shape and define masculinity among black males. If we as a nation are going to make any serious attempts to understand black males, we must generate and support more research in this area.

Because this book is only a beginning, future research in this area should be quantifiable and should seek to operationalize variables such as coolness or verbal ability. The impact of social class, education, popularity, values, abilities, and urban versus rural residence on how black males engage in cool pose should be explored with firsthand, ethnographic studies. Not only do we need more positive models that emphasize the contributions of black males, we need additional research in areas that address black masculinity and the impact of socioeconomic class on their lives. Equally important, we need more research that examines how black males make use of pride to achieve social competence.

Expand the Study of Masculinity

While the new men's studies field has focused primarily on white middle-class males, recently there have been some efforts to study culture and masculinity. For example, Kimmel and Messner use a social constructionist perspective to argue that the meaning of masculinity varies from culture to culture and that the definition of masculinity within a culture varies over time. This perspective could advance our understanding of black masculinity.

To date we know little about the cultural context within which black males learn and act out masculinity, male roles, and values. We need to know more about how they define anger, performance, impression management, social competence, control, pride, respect, and status that later lead to problematic behaviors or that help them to cope. More research is necessary if we are to attack such problems as homicide, mugging, gang behavior, crime, early pregnancy, or drug involvement (problems that black males contribute to in high proportions because of long-standing oppression). We need more insight into how black males perceive and utilize various expressions of masculinity as coping mechanisms.

Because of the emphasis black males put on performance, expressiveness, and symbolic displays, Goffman's dramaturgical analysis might be a useful framework for the study of black masculinity.

Suggestions for Social Programs, Intervention, and Policy Changes

Afrocentric Socialization

The Afrocentric model has been drawing attention in the black community as a means to educate both delinquent and nondelinquent black youths. Firmly grounded in African and African-American culture and history, Afrocentric socialization inspires black parents and adults to structure their behavior, values, and institutions in new ways. They are encouraged to teach children values emphasizing cooperation, mutual respect, commitment, and love of family, race, community, and nation.

This approach encourages blacks to define behavior that is destructive to self and others as being counterproductive to themselves and to the black community. These behaviors include compulsive masculinity, dealing in or abusing drugs, and violence.

The Afrocentric ideology is a value system based on African civilization and philosophy. It is not antiwhite, but it is an ideology that encourages black Americans to transcend their problems by reclaiming traditional African values. According to Oliver, these emphasize humanity's oneness with nature, spirituality, and collectivism. This perspective is in direct contrast to the Eurocentric world view, which encourages controlling nature, materialism, and individualism.

Afrocentrism is a collective philosophy—underpinned by meaningful cultural traditions and institutions—that will promote the growth of blacks as individuals and as members of a community. This is no less than what other American racial and ethnic groups have established to ensure their success in America. Some argue that the failure of blacks to develop such a world view before now has made them vulnerable to structural pressures that ultimately cause social problems and violence. Some observers view decay in the black community as the result of constant exposure to the Eurocentric value system. By emphasizing individualism and materialism, Eurocentric values fit neither African history nor the black experience in America.

Those who fall under the Eurocentric world view are likely to develop an acute interest in and desire for material goods—precisely the path less open to African-Americans. Historically native-born Africans have been socialized to view themselves in the context of family and social obligations to community. The Eurocentric world view neutralizes values such as unity, cooperation, and mutual respect. The Afrocentric ideology attempts to socialize children (or resocialize adults) toward values that elevate the interests of the community over those of the individual. As Oliver notes, the Afrocentric perspective helps blacks to assert themselves: "I am because we are; and since we are, therefore I am."

The model may be particularly appropriate for those black youths who have had difficulty juggling impulse control with the norms of exaggerated masculinity that have led to violence. Compulsive masculinity, self-destruction, the tough-guy role, and violence are elements of a dysfunctional adaptation to racism and discrimination. Oliver argues that blacks, especially black males, have failed to develop an Afrocentric cultural ideology or world view that could help them mitigate the adverse effects of oppression.

Manhood Training Programs

Many black males make the passage from boyhood to manhood under the tutelage of the streets and peers who define manhood in terms of toughness, sexual conquest, and thrill-seeking. Because of this pattern, the Afrocentric cultural movement in the 1980s incorporated African-style rites of passage for the socialization of young black boys.

One of the better-known programs is Paul Hill's manhood training program. The rites, based on African customs, help black boys view manhood in a way that contributes to their own positive identity as well as to survival and progress of the black community.[4] His programs train young black boys in how to be good husbands and fathers through immersion in black history, cultural enrichment, sex education, reinforcement of education, political awareness, life skills management, and community service. These elements can promote understanding of the behaviors that make positive contributions to the black community and those that cause decay.

The Hares, in *Bringing the Black Boys to Manhood: The Passage*, report that the purpose of manhood training for young black boys is to teach them a sense of responsibility, personal mastery, and a commitment to family, race, community, and country.

Karenga believes, and Oliver concurs, that high rates of social problems and violence among blacks could be reduced if black parents were to teach their children the Afrocentric value system he calls *Nguzo Saba*. There are seven core values of Nguzo Saba:

Umoja—unity in family, race, community and nation;

Kujichagulia—self-determination, or defining ourselves, rather than allowing one's culture to be defined by others;

Ujima—collective work and responsibility;

Ujamma—cooperative economics, perhaps through development of black-owned businesses;

Nia—purpose, or a desire to understand how the dominant society uses racism and discrimination to oppress blacks;

Kuumba—creativity, or the desire and need to contribute to the aesthetic quality of black life; and

Imani—faith, the internalization of Afrocentric values.

These stand as minimum core values necessary to reconstruct the black community, but must be understood within the context of society-wide efforts to alleviate poverty and discrimination.

Direct Intervention with Individuals

Many organizations and institutions have sponsored creative intervention/prevention programs for delinquent and emotionally troubled black youths who experience problems with impulse control and exaggerated forms of masculinity. These programs encourage impulse management and offer life skills, values and vocational training, placement counseling, and remedial education.

One program described by Sanders is the 21st Century Leadership Camp, founded in Selma, Alabama, which grew out of the black community's conviction that leaders for tomorrow must be developed from among the youths of today, regardless of poverty, brushes with delinquency, boredom with school, or failed educational and social service systems. Similar leadership camps have sprung up in other states; all focus on developing children's pride, self-respect, and leadership skills, but always within the context of what is best for their communities.

Other successful and innovative programs are the National Urban League's Black Male Responsibility Program, City Lights, The Door, and the Junior Citizens Corp. Others utilize mentoring, conflict-resolution, manhood training, and dialectical therapy.[5]

Mancini has suggested that, because a person's style emerges prior to junior high school and crystallizes during adolescence, intervention efforts should be attempted early and should include careful analysis of interpersonal styles, including coolness. This would allow youth workers, parents, and teachers a framework that "goes beyond personality traits, specific acts of deviance, or demographic characteristics [such as poverty or inner-city residence], and focuses on how a young person attempts to cope with competing pressures and messages from others in his environment."[6]

Formation of National Policy Groups

The National Council of African American Men (NCAAM)—the first black male umbrella group in the United States—was founded recently by Richard Majors and Jacob Gordon to address the problems of black males in America. Among other agenda items, NCAAM will develop a clearinghouse and think tank designed to educate the public on the critical issues facing black men in America and to help solve problems and shape public policy. NCAAM also plans to create a special task force on education in order to address the high rate of suspensions and dropouts among black youths. It will review germane research on these problems and develop action and support programs in our nation's schools.

The Council on Black Youth Affairs, part of NCAAM, will implement and oversee such innovative programs as mentoring, manhood training programs, the Adopt-a-Black-Male Volunteer Program (five percent of income and five hours per week), life skills training, and the Black Youth Leadership Symposium (based at the University of Kansas, Kansas City). NCAAM has also founded the *Journal of African American Studies* (focused on black males).

Other national forums for research, discussion, and policy recommendations for positive change and empowerment are the National Black Family Summit, the Children's Defense Fund, the National Black Child Development Institute, and the National Council of Negro Women, to name a few.

More Responsive and Effective Schools

Earlier, we identified the revolving door of education for blacks and their greater chances of being failed, suspended, and rerouted into special education classes, or of dropping out altogether. Many solutions have been attempted. Certainly continued efforts to desegregate schools and ensure equal opportunity for all black children must not falter. Schools that house predominantly black pupils should not pay the penalty of being assigned less experienced teachers or receiving lower per-pupil expenditures.

Linkages between high schools and institutions of higher education that facilitate and encourage high school completion and college entrance—for example, the long-standing and very successful Upward Bound program—should continue to be supported.

Racial awareness films, plays, discussions, and seminars should be part of every school's curriculum at various developmental levels. Some schools might encourage teachers to participate in Afrocentric preservice and in-service training. Such programs should be viewed as essentials, not luxuries.

The national movement toward school-based management that includes serious input from teachers, students, and parents, as well as administrators and school committees, is aimed toward empowering all students. The impact for historically disempowered groups, such as blacks, should be especially notable.

School curricula should be infused with African and African-American history and culture. This would help reduce stereotypes, biases, and misconceptions toward blacks. Until funding and other support for quality public education is defined as a pressing priority by federal, state, and local governments, however, curricular and management initiatives will have little impact.

Racial Awareness Workshops

Intensive workshops on race relations and cultural differences should be conducted on-site during regular working hours as part of routine in-service training for all professionals. Workshops in educational settings should involve parents, students, and teachers participating in role-playing, discussion of case studies, and group techniques for values' exploration.

Helping professionals understand how and why some black males use cool behaviors and helping blacks see where contrasting definitions of behavior may occur could enhance race relations. Educators, mental health professionals, teachers, psychologists, prison officials, and social workers should all have an in-depth knowledge of how the black male is likely to define his masculinity; cool pose is an integral part of that masculine identity. Racial and gender identity theory should be an integral part of professional education.

We hope that this book stimulates research to help address these and other questions. However, all efforts toward broadening research or writing new social policy must be clear about several issues. First, exploring black responses to oppression must be cast in terms of cultural distinctiveness, not cultural or individual pathology. Second, recognition of cultural distinctiveness cannot be construed as a way to avoid making substantial changes in the structure of our society. And third, social policies and programs must have the full support of all segments of society, not just those who have fallen victim to its fundamental failings.

As Burnham and others succinctly argue, institutional racism and massive economic and social disparities have forced minorities into crisis; to focus on individual pathologies (such as drug abuse, dropping out, or criminality) only serves to perpetuate the crisis.

In Closing: A Man's Mind Is His Castle

Cool pose is a coping mechanism par excellence that some black males have learned to use to help counter social inequality. As long as they experience discrimination (or there is a perception of discrimination), there will be the need for coolness. African-American males in this country have had relatively little support to help them cope with life crises. Their minds have been their primary line of defense.

In this country we say, "a man's home is his castle." However, it is tragic that the masses of black men have no castle to protect. Their minds have become their psychological castle, defended by impenetrable cool. Cool pose is the bittersweet symbol of a socially disesteemed group that shouts, "we are," in the face of a hostile and indifferent world that everywhere screams, "you are not."

Cool pose has gained ideological legitimacy in the black community. It is part of a social reality that cuts across all socioeconomic groups as black men fight to preserve a modicum of dignity, pride, respect, and masculinity.

The black man desires the most ordinary of successes: a steady job, the chance to be a productive citizen and provide for his family, a chance to help shape the direction and future of his country, and to be able to live in peace. He wants the opportunity to be himself and have the chance to better his life and the lives of those he loves. Cool pose protects the castle of his mind. His instinct to mask and stay detached in the face of likely failure guides his bids to achieve what others would see as routine success. His dreams, just as fireworks on the most American of July days, burst in splendid shows of color and force. It is time for those dreams to become reality.

The Helping Soul

I believe I am because I am.
I believe I can because I can be me.
I believe I can be me because what I do is my very best.
It may not be yours, but it is mine
—and this is the most important thing to me.
But what I ask most is for you to let me grow and mature
without bothering or hindering me
—because this way I become naturally what I really am.
And you know that this is the best gift the world could give me.

And in result things are so beautiful like this.
It's like the races of mankind.
Everybody has his own color and beautiful ways and also its own
culture, which makes it all the more colorful.
And you know I believe I am somebody,
because I believe one day everyone
will believe they can if they let themselves be
—I can be—I believe I can be . . . and will.
All you have to do is love me
and, World, I will love you forever.

—Richard Majors

Notes

Chapter 1. Cool Pose: Expression and Survival

1. For a full theoretical exploration of the concept of cool pose see Larabee 1986; Majors 1983, 1986, 1987, 1990, 1991; Majors and Nikelly 1983; Nikelly and Majors 1986; Ridley 1984; and Wiley 1990. See also Mancini 1981.
2. Interviews conducted by Majors with "Phil" constituted the central data for Majors' dissertation (1987); interviews with "Leroy" were conducted by black male staff members of the Pathways to Identity project at Harvard University and were included in Mancini's *Strategic Styles: Coping in the Inner City* (1981).
3. Pettigrew 1964, 28.
4. Ibid.
5. Phillips 1971, 154–158.

Chapter 2. Social Stress and Social Symptoms

1. From the recording "Lonesome Train," by Earl Robinson, text by Millard Lampell with Odetta and Brock Peters (United Artists #604).
2. W. J. Wilson 1990, 8.
3. Extensive literature exists comparing the prevalence of mental disorders among blacks and whites in the United States (Kleiner et al. 1973; Passamanick 1963; Sharpley 1977; Bulhan 1985a). There is some controversy as to whether psychopathology reflects actual disorder or patterns of inequity in services and professional bias.
4. Bulhan 1985a, 371–72.
5. Williams 1986.
6. Matney and Johnson 1983.
7. Gibbs 1988.
8. Matney and Johnson 1983.
9. National Center for Health Statistics 1985.
10. *St. Paul Pioneer Press* 1991; *Newsweek* 1991.
11. Heckler 1985; McCord and Freeman 1990; Cordes 1985.
12. Hampton 1987.
13. Gibbs 1988; U.S. Bureau of the Census 1975.
14. Gibbs 1988, 258–261.

15. Gibbs 1988.
16. Gite 1985, 25. In general, though, white males recorded the highest suicide rate (20.0 per 100,000), followed by black males (11.6), white females (6.6), and black females (2.8) (Johnson and Johnson 1986, 218).
17. Reported in Gite 1985.
18. Heckler 1985, 75.
19. Gibbs 1988, 280; Gary 1986.
20. Gibbs 1988, 8–10.
21. Hampton 1987.
22. Oliver 1988, 1989a; Bureau of Justice Statistics 1985.
23. Clark 1980; Stewart and Scott 1978; see also Gary 1984, 13.

Chapter 3. Cool Pose and Masculinity

1. Folb 1980, 126.
2. Glasgow 1980, 96–99.
3. Cazenave 1981, 176–78.
4. Keil 1966, 22.
5. Cazenave 1981, 179.
6. Cazenave 1981.
7. Milner 1972, 114–15.
8. Folb 1980, 121–22.

Chapter 4. In Search of Pride and Manhood

1. Mancini 1981, 163–64.
2. Dworkin and Dworkin, 6.
3. Pettigrew 1964, 50–51.
4. Fordham and Ogbu 1986, 179.
5. Gaston 1986, 372–73.
6. Della Cava 1989; Stewart 1989.
7. *USA Today*, two-part series on L.A. gangs, December 7–8, 1989.

Chapter 5. The Genesis of Black Masking

1. Wright 1964, 17–18.
2. Nielson 1977, 126.
3. Cited in Young 1972, 173.
4. Levine 1977.
5. Langston Hughes in White 1984, 32–33.

Chapter 6. The Expressive Life-Style

1. Mancini 1981, 4.
2. Mancini 1981, 23.

3. Folb 1980, 109.
4. Cooke [1972] 1980; Johnson 1971; Majors 1991.
5. These are elaborated upon in Majors 1991.
6. Johnson 1971, 185.
7. Johnson 1971, 186. This section also benefitted from the work of Hannah 1984; Rich 1974; Cooke 1980; Barnes 1988.
8. Smith 1983; Hannah 1984; LaFrance 1974; Shuter 1979.
9. Rosenwald 1984; Cox 1984; Grubb 1984.

Chapter 7. The Cool Cat Life-Style

1. Firestone 1957, 5.
2. Mancini 1981, 164.
3. Folb 1980, 109–10; see also Knapp 1978 and Majors 1987, 1991.
4. Ibid.
5. Dworkin and Dworkin, 2–3.
6. Folb 1980, 112, 115.
7. Folb 1980, 38.
8. Folb 1980, 42.
9. Brown 1969.
10. McCord et al. 1969, 129.

Chapter 8. Playing the Dozens

1. Grier and Cobbs 1971.
2. McCormick in Foster 1974, 212. For other discussions of the dozens, see Foster 1974, 215–16; Merwin 1960, 295; and Brewer 1966, 32.
3. Cited in Kochman 1972, 205.
4. Cited in Rainwater 1970, 278.
5. Brown 1972, 25–27.
6. Levine 1977, 350.
7. Abrahams and Gay 1972, 201.
8. Guffy 1971, 48.

Chapter 9. Summary and Implications

1. Dee 1983, 88, 90, 92.
2. Taylor 1985, 57.
3. Ibid.
4. Oliver 1989. See also Fair 1977; Kunjufu 1983, 1986; Hare and Hare 1985; Perkins 1986.
5. Gibbs 1988; Balcazar et al. 1990; Spivak et al. 1989; De La Cancela 1986.
6. Mancini Billson 1988, 531–32.

Other Work on Cool

Even though coolness is a universal phenomenon, cool as a legitimate area of research has been virtually ignored by social scientists. Perhaps cool has not been taken very seriously and has been slow to develop as a research area because of the term's association with slang.

Discussion of cool in psychology books has seldom warranted more than one or two paragraphs. Many major books on personality and ego development of African-American males have failed to include cool in the index at all: *The Psychology of Blacks: An Afro-American Perspective* (White 1984); *Black Psychology* (Jones 1980); *Psychology and the Black Experience*, (Pugh 1972); *Black Men* (Gary 1984); *The Mark of Oppression* (Kardiner and Ovesey 1951); *Black Americans* (Baughman 1971); and *The Psychology of the Afro-American: A Humanistic Approach* (Jenkins 1982).

We located only a handful of articles or manuscripts with the word cool in the title: "Coolness in Everyday Life" (Lyman and Scott 1970); "Time and Cool People" (Horton 1970); "Digging, Being Cool, Doing Your Thing (Not Necessarily In That Order)" (in Abrahams 1976); and "Cool: Young Adults in the Negro Ghetto" (Dworkin and Dworkin).

Sociology, sociolinguistics, anthropology, and music (the cool period in jazz music) should be credited with making the best effort toward understanding cool. Some of the more informative works that discuss cool are Perkins (1975), Glasgow (1980), Hannerz (1969b), Schulz (1969), Lyman and Scott (1970), and Kochman (1970).

Scholarly works in anthropology that index cool as a subject include *Talking Black* (Abrahams 1976); *Positively Black* (Abrahams 1970); *Coming Up Black* (Schulz 1969); and *Rappin' and Stylin' Out* (Kochman 1972a; cool as a subject is not indexed but is cited because of two influential papers that discuss cool behaviors: Horton's "Time and Cool People" and Kochman's "Toward an Ethnography of Black American Speech Behavior").

The first sociological work to devote an entire chapter to the Cool Guy was in *Strategic Styles: Coping in the Inner City* (Mancini 1981). Other sociological works that index cool as a subject are *The Black Underclass: Poverty, Unemployment, and Entrapment of*

Ghetto Youth (Glasgow 1980), and *Lifestyles in the Black Ghetto* (McCord, Howard, Friedberg, and Harwood 1969). This research has tended to be descriptive rather than analytical.

In addition, "indigenous works" by those who have lived in the nation's inner cities have made significant, descriptive contributions to our understanding of cool and the daily experiences of poor black males. These include literary works by Gwaltney 1980; Brown 1965; Haley and Malcolm X 1964; Wright 1937, 1940, 1964; Gaines 1972, 1973; Beck 1969; and Thomas 1967. More recent contributions are cited after each chapter of our book.

Bibliography

Abrahams, R. 1962. Playing the dozens. *Journal of American Folklore* 75:209–20.
———. 1964. Verbal contest and creativity. In *Deep down in the jungle*, ed. R. Abrahams. Chicago: Aldine.
———. 1970. *Positively black.* Englewood Cliffs, NJ: Prentice-Hall.
———. 1976. *Talking black.* Newbury, MA: Rawley House.
Abrahams, R., and G. Gay. 1972. Black culture in the classroom. In *Language and cultural diversity in American education*, ed. R. Abrahams and R. Troike. Englewood Cliffs, NJ: Prentice-Hall.
Ames, R. 1950. Protest and irony in Negro folklore. *Science and Society* 14:193–213.

Balcazar, F. E., R. G. Majors, et al. (In press). Teaching minority high school students to recruit helpers to attain personal and educational goals. *Journal of Behavioral Education.*
Baldwin, J. 1962. *Another country.* New York: Dial Press.
———. 1963. *The fire next time.* New York: Dial Press.
———. 1961. *Nobody knows my name.* New York: Dial Press.
Barnes, 1988, telephone conversation.
Bascom, W. 1969. *The Yoruba of southwestern Nigeria.* New York: Holt, Rinehart, & Winston.
Baughman, E. 1971. *Black Americans: A psychological analysis.* New York: Academic Press.
Beck, R. 1969. *Pimp: The story of my life.* Los Angeles: Holloway House.
Berdie, R. 1947. Playing the dozens. *Journal of Abnormal and Social Psychiatry* 42:120–21.
Billingsley, A. 1968. *Black families in white America.* Englewood Cliffs, NJ: Prentice-Hall.
Bonham, F. 1972. *Cool cat.* New York: Random House.
Boykins, W. 1983. The academic performance of Afro-American children. In *Achievement and achievement motives*, ed. J. Spence. San Francisco: W. H. Freeman.
Brewer, J. 1966, December 5. Hidden language—ghetto children know what they're talking about. *New York Times Magazine* (5 Dec):32–35.
Brown, C. 1965. *Manchild in the promised land.* New York: Macmillan.
Brown, H. R. 1969. *Die nigger die!* New York: Dial Press.

————. 1972. Street talk. In *Rappin' and stylin' out*, ed. T. Kochman (pp. 205–208). Urbana: University of Illinois Press.

Bulhan, H. 1985a. Black Americans and psychopathology: An overview of research and therapy. *Psychotherapy* 22:370–78.

————. 1985b. *Frantz Fanon and the psychology of oppression*. New York: Plenum.

Bureau of Justice Statistics. 1985. *The prevalence of imprisonment*. Washington, D.C.: U.S. Department of Justice.

Burnham, M., et al. Scapegoating the black family: Black women speak. 1989. *The Nation* (July 24/31).

Cazenave, N. 1981. Black men in America: The quest for manhood. In *Black Families*, ed. H. P. McAdoo. Beverly Hills, CA: Sage.

————. 1979. Middle-income black fathers: An analysis of the provider role. *The Family Coordinator* 28:583–93.

————. 1984. Race, socioeconomic status, and age: The social context of American masculinity. *Sex Roles* 11:639–57.

Chimezie, A. 1976. The dozens: An African-heritage theory. *Journal of Black Studies* 6:401–20.

Clark, K. 1980. The role of race. *New York Times Magazine* (Oct):25–35.

Cooke, B. 1980. Nonverbal communication among Afro-Americans: An initial classification. In *Black psychology*, 2nd ed., ed. R. L. Jones. New York: Harper & Row.

Cordes, C. 1985. Black males at risk in America. *APA Monitor*, January.

Cox, D. 1984. Brooklyn's furious rockers: Break dance roots in a breakneck neighborhood. *Dance Magazine*.

Dee, R. 1983. What's right about black men? A praise song for the elegance of the black male spirit. *Ebony* (Aug).

De La Cancela, V. 1986. A critical analysis of Puerto Rican machismo: Implications for clinical practice. *Psychotherapy* 23:291–96.

Della Cava, M. 1989. L.A. fights back. *USA Today* (8 Dec).

Dollard, J. 1939. The dozens: Dialectic of insult. *American Imago* 1:3–25.

Dove, A. 1968. Soul story. *New York Times Magazine* (8 Dec:38–41).

Dubbert, J. 1979. *A man's place: Masculinity in transition*. Englewood Cliffs, NJ: Prentice-Hall.

Dunbar, P. 1972. We wear the mask. In *Black experience*, ed. C. Young. San Rafael, CA: LeWing Press.

Dworkin, B., and S. Dworkin. *Cool: Young adults in the Negro ghetto*. Unpublished manuscript, Washington University, St. Louis, MO.

Ellis, H., and S. Newman. 1972. The greaser is a "bad ass"; the growster is a "mutha": An analysis of two urban youth roles. In *Rappin, and stylin' out*, ed. T. Kochman. Urbana: University of Illinois Press.

Ellison, R. 1960 (1947). *Invisible man*. New York: Signet Books.

Fair, F. 1977. *Orita for black youth: An invitation into Christian adulthood.* Valley Forge, PA: Judson Press.

Fanon, F. 1967. Negroes and whites and rates of mental illness: Reconsideration of a myth. *Psychiatry* 32:428–46.

Farley, R. 1989. Trends in the residential segregation of social and economic groups among American blacks: 1970 to 1980. Paper presented at the Conference on the Truly Disadvantaged. Northwestern University, Evanston, Illinois, October.

Firestone, H. 1957. Cats, kicks and color. *Social Problems* 5:3–13.

Folb, E. 1980. *Runnin' down some lines: The language and culture of black teenagers.* Cambridge, MA: Harvard University Press.

Fordham, S., and J.U. Ogbu. 1986. Black students' school success: Coping with the "burden of 'acting white.' " *The Urban Review* 18:176–206.

Foster, H. 1974. *Ribbin', jivin' and playin' the dozens: The unrecognized dilemma of inner city schools.* Cambridge, MA: Ballinger Publishing Co.

Franklin, C. 1984. Black male-black female conflict: Individually caused and culturally nurtured. *Journal of Black Studies* 15:139–54.

Frazier, E. F. 1940. *Negro youth at the crossways.* Washington, D.C.: American Council on Education.

Gary, L. 1984. *Black men.* Beverly Hills, CA: Sage.

———. 1986. Drinking, homicide, and the black male. *Journal of Black Studies* 17:15–29.

Gaston, J. 1986. The destruction of the young black male: The impact of popular culture and organized sports. *Journal of Black Studies* 16:369–84.

Gibbs, J. T. 1988. *Young, black, and male in America: An endangered species.* Dover, MA: Auburn House.

Gite, L. 1985. Black men and stress. *Essence* (Nov).

Glasgow, D. 1980. *The black underclass: Poverty, unemployment, and entrapment of ghetto youth.* San Francisco: Jossey-Bass.

Goffman, E. 1959. *The presentation of self in everyday life.* New York: Doubleday.

Goines, D. 1972. *Whoreson: The story of a ghetto pimp.* Los Angeles: Holloway House.

———. 1973. *Street player.* Los Angeles: Holloway House.

Grier, W. H., and P. M. Cobbs. 1968. *Black rage.* New York: Bantam Books.

———. 1971. *The Jesus bag.* New York: McGraw-Hill.

Grubb, K. 1984. His-hippin' in the South Bronx. Lester Wilson's beat street. *Dance Magazine* 58:76–78.

Guffy, O. 1971. *Ossie: The autobiography of a black woman.* New York: W. W. Norton.

Guterman, S. ed. 1972. *Black psyche.* Berkeley, CA: The Glendessary Press.

Gwaltney, J. 1980. *Drylongo: A self-portrait of black America.* New York: Random House.

Haley, A., and Malcolm X. 1964. *The autobiography of Malcolm X.* New York: Grove Press.

Hammond, E. 1965. The contest system: A survival technique. Ph.D. diss., Washington University. St. Louis, MO.

Hampton, R. L. 1987. *Violence in the black family: Correlates and consequences.* Lexington, MA: Lexington Books.

Hannah, J. L. 1984. Black/white nonverbal differences, dance and dissonance: Implications for desegregation. In *Nonverbal behavior: Perspectives, applications, intercultural insight*, ed. A. Wolfgang. Lewiston, NY: C. J. Hogrefe.

Hannerz, U. 1969a. Roots of black manhood. *Transaction* 6:12–24.

———. 1969b. *Soulside: Inquiries into ghetto culture and community.* New York: Columbia University Press.

———. 1970. Another look at lower-class black culture. In *Soul*, ed. L. Rainwater. Chicago: Aldine.

Hare, N., and J. Hare. 1985. *Bringing the black boy to manhood: The passage.* San Francisco: The Black Think Tank.

Heckler, M. 1985. *Report of the Secretary's task force on black and minority health.* Bethesda, MD: U.S. Department of Health and Human Services.

Hill, M., and T. Ackiss. 1943. Social class: A frame of reference for the study of Negro society. *Social Forces* 22:92–106.

Holt, G. 1972. Inversion in the black community. In *Rappin' and stylin' out*, ed. T. Kochman. Urbana, IL: University of Illinois Press.

Horton, J. 1970. Time and cool people. In *Soul*, ed. L. Rainwater. Chicago: Aldine.

Hudson, J. 1972. The hustling ethic. In *Rappin' and stylin' out*, ed. T. Kochman. Urbana, IL: University of Illinois Press.

Hughes, L. 1961. *The best of Simple.* New York: Hill and Wang.

Huizinga, J. 1955. *Homo ludens: A study of the play element in culture.* Boston: Beacon Press.

Jacob, J. 1986. An overview of black America in 1985. In *The state of black America.* New York: National Urban League.

Janzen, John. (May, 1989). Personal communication.

Jenkins, A. 1982. *The psychology of the Afro-American: A humanistic approach.* New York: Pergamon Press.

Johnson, K. R. 1971. Black kinesics: Some nonverbal communication patterns in black culture. *Florida Foreign Language Reporter* 9:95–122.

Johnson, B., and J. Johnson. 1980. *Black resource guide.* Washington, D.C.: B. Johnson and J. Johnson.

Jones, L. 1963. *Blues people.* New York: Morrow Quill.

Jones, R. ed. 1980. *Black psychology*, 2nd ed. New York: Harper & Row.

Kardiner, A., and L. Ovesey. 1951. *The mark of oppression: A psychological study of the American Negro.* New York: W.W. Norton.

Karenga, R. 1977. *Kwanzaa: Origins, concepts, practice.* Los Angeles: Kawaida Publications.

Keil, C. 1966. *Urban blues.* Chicago: University of Chicago Press.

Keiser, L. 1972. Roles and ideologies. In *Rappin' and stylin' out*, ed. T. Kochman. Urbana, IL: University of Illinois Press.

Kimmel, M. S., and M. A. Messner. 1989. *Men's lives*. New York: Macmillan.

Kleiner, R., J. Tuckman, and M. LaVell. 1960. Mental disorders and status based on race. *Psychiatry* 23:271–74.

Knapp, M. L. 1978. The field of nonverbal communication: An overview. In *On speech communication: An anthology of contemporary writings and messages*, ed. C. J. Stewart and B. Kendall. New York: Holt, Rinehart & Winston.

Kochman, T. 1970. Rapping in the ghetto. In *Soul*, ed. L. Rainwater. Chicago: Aldine.

———, ed. 1972a. *Rappin' and stylin' out*. Urbana, IL: University of Illinois Press.

———. 1972b. Toward an ethnography of black America. In *Rappin' and stylin' out*, ed. T. Kochman. Urbana, IL: University of Illinois Press.

———. 1981. *Black and white styles in conflict*. Chicago: The University of Chicago Press.

Kunjufu, J. 1983. *Countering the conspiracy to destroy black boys*. Chicago: The University of Chicago Press.

———. 1986. *Countering the conspiracy to destroy black boys*. Chicago: African American Images.

LaFrance, M. 1974. Nonverbal cues to conversational turn taking between black speakers. Paper presented at the annual meeting of the American Psychological Association, New Orleans.

Larabee, M. 1986. Helping reluctant black males: An affirmation approach. *Journal of Multicultural Counseling and Development* 14:25–37.

Lefever, H. 1981. Playing the dozens: A mechanism for social control. *Phylon* 42:73–85.

Levine, L. 1977. *Black culture and black consciousness*. New York: Oxford University Press.

Liebow, E. 1967. *Tally's corner*. Boston: Little, Brown.

Lyman, S. M., and M. B. Scott. 1970. Coolness in everyday life. In *A sociology of the absurd*, ed. S. M. Lyman and M. B. Scott. New York: Appleton-Century-Crofts.

Majors, R. 1979. The helping soul. In *American collegiate poets: Falls concours*, ed. V. Churillo (p. 172). Los Angeles: International Publications.

———. 1983. Cool pose: A new hypothesis in understanding anti-social behavior in lower socioeconomic status males. Unpublished manuscript, University of Illinois, Urbana, IL.

———. 1986. Cool pose: The proud signature of black survival. *Changing Men: Issues in Gender, Sex and Politics* 17:5–6.

———. 1987. Cool pose: A new approach toward a systematic understanding and studying of black male behavior. Unpublished Ph.D. diss., University of Illinois, Urbana, IL.

————. 1989. Cool pose: The proud signature of black survival. In *Men's lives*, ed. M. S. Kimmel and M. A. Messner. New York: Macmillan.

————. 1990. Cool pose: Black masculinity and sport. In *Critical perspectives on sport, men and masculinity*, ed. M. A. Messner and D. Sabo. Champaign, IL: Human Kinetics.

————. 1991. Nonverbal behavior and communication styles among African Americans. In R. Jones, ed., *Black psychology*, 3rd ed. Berkeley, CA: Cobb and Henry.

————, and A. Nikelly. 1983. Serving the black minority: A new direction for psychotherapy. *Journal of Non-White Concerns* 11:142–51.

Mancini, J. K. 1981. *Strategic styles: Coping in the inner city*. Hanover, NH: University Press of New England.

————Billson. 1988. Fostering nondeviant lifestyles against the odds: Toward a clinical sociological model of intervention strategies. *Adolescence* 23:517–32.

Matney, W., and D. Johnson, eds. 1983. *America's black population 1970–1982: A statistical view*. Washington, D.C.: U.S. Department of Commerce, Bureau of Census, U.S. Government Printing Office.

McCord, C., and H. Freeman. 1990. Excessive mortality in Harlem. *New England Journal of Medicine* 322:173–77.

McCord, W., J. Howard, B. Friedberg, and E. Harwood. 1969. *Life styles in the black ghetto*. New York: W. W. Norton.

McCormick, W. 1974. In *Ribbin', jivin' and playin' the dozens: The unrecognized dilemma of inner city schools*, ed. H. Foster (p. 212). Cambridge, MA: Ballinger.

Merton, R. K. 1957. *Social theory and social structure*. New York: The Free Press.

Merwin, D. J. 1960. *Reaching the fighting gang*. New York: New York City Youth Board.

Miller, W. 1959. *The cool world*. Boston: Little, Brown.

Milner, R. 1972. The trickster, the bad nigger, and the new urban ethnography: An initial report and editorial coda. *Urban Life and Culture* 1:109–17.

Moynihan, D. P. 1967. *The Negro family: The case for national action*. Washington, D.C.: U.S. Government Printing Office.

Myrdal, G. 1962. *An American dilemma*. New York: Harper & Row.

National Center for Health Statistics. 1985. Advanced report of final natality statistics, 1983. *Monthly Vital Statistics* 34, supplement 2.

Neissen, U. 1986. *The school achievement of minority children*. Hillsdale, NJ: Lawrence Erlbaum Associates.

Newsweek. 1991. Twenty percent of the total U.S. deployment in the Gulf are Blacks. (11 Mar).

Nielson, D. 1977. *Black ethos*. Westport, CT: Greenwood Press.

Nikelly, A., and R. Majors. 1986. Technique for counseling black students. *Techniques: A Journal for Remedial Education and Counseling* 2:48–54.

Oliver, W. 1984. Black males and the tough guy image: A dysfunctional compensatory adaptation. *The Western Journal of Black Studies* 8:201–2.

———. 1988. The symbolic display of compulsive masculinity in the lower-class black bar. Unpublished manuscript, University of Delaware, Newark, DE.

———. 1989a. Sexual conquest and patterns of black-on-black violence: A structural-cultural perspective. *Violence and Victims* 4:4.

———. 1989b. Black males and social problems: Prevention through Afrocentric socialization. *Journal of Black Studies* 20:15–39.

Okolo, C. 1974. *Racism: A philosophic probe.* Jericho, NY: Exposition Press.

Osgood, C. 1940. Ingalik material culture. London: Oxford University Press.

Parker, W. Cultural and academic stress imposed on Afro-Americans: Implications for educational change. Unpublished manuscript, Educational Testing Service, Princeton, NJ.

Passamanick, B. 1963. Some misconceptions concerning differences in the racial prevalence of mental diseases. *American Journal of Orthopsychiatry* 33:72–86.

Perkins, E. 1975. *Home is a dirty street: The social oppression of black children.* Chicago: Third World Press.

———. 1986. *Harvesting new generations: The positive development of black youth.* Chicago: Third World Press.

Pettigrew, T. 1964. *A profile of the Negro American.* Princeton, NJ: D. Van Nostrand.

Phillips, W. 1971. The survival techniques of black Americans. In *Black life and culture in the United States,* ed. R. Goldstein. New York: Thomas Y. Crowell.

Pinkney, A. 1984. *The myth of black progress.* New York: Cambridge University Press.

Poussaint, A. 1967. Negro self-hate. *New York Times Magazine* (20 Aug:52).

Pugh, R. 1972. *Psychology and the black experience.* Monterey, CA: Brooks/Cole.

Rainwater, L. 1966. The crucible of identity: The lower-class Negro family. *Daedalus* 95:172–216.

———. 1970a. *Behind ghetto walls: Black families in a federal slum.* Chicago: Aldine.

———. 1970b. *Soul.* Chicago: Aldine.

Rich, A. L. 1974. *Interracial communication.* New York: Harper & Row.

Ridley, C. 1984. Clinical treatment of the nondisclosing black client: A therapeutic paradox. *American Psychologist* 39:1234–44.

Robinson, I.E., W. C. Bailey, and J. M. Smith. 1985. Self-perception of the husband/father in the intact lower class black family. *Phylon* 46:136–47.

Rose, H.M., and P.D. McClain. 1990. *Race, place and risk: Black homicide in urban America.* Ithaca, NY: State University of New York Press.

Rosenwald, P. 1984. Breaking away '80s style. *Dance Magazine.*

Sanders, R. M. 1991. 21st century leaders: A model program in the black community. *Future Choices: Toward a National Youth Policy* 2:107–09.

Schulz, D. 1969. *Coming up black: Patterns of ghetto specialization.* Englewood Cliffs, NJ: Prentice-Hall.

Sharpley, R. 1977. *Treatment issues: Foreign medical graduate and black patient populations.* Cambridge, MA: The Solomon Fuller Institute.

Shuter, R. 1979. Gaze behavior in interracial and intra-racial interaction. In *Intercultural communication annual,* ed. N. C. Jain. Falls Church, VA: Speech Communication Association.

Smith, R. 1958. The unknowable Negro. In *Race: Individual and collective behaviors,* eds. E. T. Thompson and E. C. Hughes. New York: The Free Press.

Smith, A. 1983. Nonverbal communication among black female dyads: An assessment of intimacy, gender and race. *Journal of Social Issues* 39:55–67.

Snyder, M. 1987. *Public appearance/private realities: The psychology of self-monitoring behaviors.* New York: W.H. Freeman.

Spivak, H., A. J. Hausman, and D. Prothrow-Stith. 1989. Practitioner's Forum: Public health and the primary prevention of adolescent violence—the Violence Prevention Project. *Violence and Victims* 4:203–11.

Squitieri, T. 1989. Just another night in gangland USA. *USA Today* (8 Dec).

St. Paul Pioneer Press. 1991. (24 Jan).

Stanback, M., and B. Pearce. 1981. Talking to "the man": Some communication strategies used by members of "subordinate social groups." *The Quarterly Journal of Speech* 67:21–30.

Stanlaw, J., and A. Peskin. 1988. Black visibility in a multiethnic high school. In *Class, race and gender in U.S. schools,* ed. L. Weis. Albany: Suny Press.

Staples, R. 1972. Race and masculinity: The dual dilemma of black men. In *Black masculinity,* ed. R. Staples. San Francisco: The Black Scholars Press.

Stewart, J., and J. Scott. 1978. The institutional decimation of black American males. *Western Journal of Black Studies* 2:82–93.

Stewart, S. A. 1989. For drug dealing PBGs, gang is "better than family." *USA Today* (7 Dec).

Straus, Murray et al. 1980. *Behind closed doors: Violence in the American family.* Garden City, N.Y.: Anchor.

Sutler, A. 1972. Playing a cold game: Phases of a ghetto career. *Urban Life and Culture* 1:77–91.

Swinton, D. 1986. Economic status of blacks in 1985. In *The state of black Americans,* ed. J. Williams. New York: National Urban League.

Taylor, R. 1977. Socialization to the black male role. In *The black male in America,* ed. D. Wilkinson and R. Taylor. Chicago: Nelson-Hall.

———. 1981. Psychological modes of adaptation. In *Black men,* ed. L. Gary. Beverly Hills, CA: Sage Publications.

Taylor, S. 1985. Give the man a hand. *Essence* (Nov):57.

Thomas, P. 1967. *Down these mean streets.* New York: Alfred A. Knopf.

Thompson, R. F. 1983. *Flash of the spirit.* New York: Random House.

U.S. Bureau of the Census. 1975. *The social and economic status of the black population in the United States. Washington, D.C.: U.S. Government Printing Office.*

Vontress, C. 1976. Racial and ethnic barriers in counseling. In *Counseling across culture*, ed. P. Pedersen, W. Lonner, and J. Draguns. Honolulu: University Press of Hawaii.

Washington, R. 1976. Toward a theory of ethnicity and social competence. Unpublished manuscript, University of Wisconsin, Milwaukee, WI.

Weis, L. 1985. *Between two worlds: Black students in an urban community college*. Boston: Routledge & Kegan Paul.

White, J. 1984. *The psychology of blacks: An Afro-American perspective*. Englewood Cliffs, NJ: Prentice-Hall.

Wiley, E. 1990. Coolposing: Misinterpreted expressions often lead to educational deprivation. *Black issues in higher education* (22 Nov).

Wilkinson, D., and R. Taylor, eds. 1977. *The black male in America*. Chicago: Nelson-Hall.

Williams, J., ed. 1986. The state of black America. New York: National Urban League.

Wilson, N.A. 1978. An overview: Language, cultural determinism and "black mythology." In *The developmental psychology of the black child*, ed. N. A. Wilson. New York: Africana Research Publication.

Wilson, W.J. 1990. Social theory and the public agenda research: The challenge of studying inner-city social dislocations. Presidential address, Annual Meeting of the American Sociological Association, Washington, DC, August.

Wright, R. 1937. *Black boy*. New York: Harper & Row.

———. 1940. *Native son*. New York: Harper & Row.

———. 1964. *White man listen!* Garden City, NY: Doubleday.

Young, C., ed. 1972. *Black experience*. San Rafael, CA: Les Wing Press.

Young, E. 1986. Time for the young lions to take over. *Pittsburgh Post-Gazette* (28 May):23.

Index

Muhammad Ali, 77
Murphy, Eddie, 4

National Black Family Summit,
114
National Black Child Develop-
ment Institute, 114
National Council of Negro
Women, 114
National Council of African
American Men, 114
National Urban League, Black
Male Responsibility Program,
113
Native Americans, life expectancy,
19
Nguzo Saba, 112–113
Nigeria, 57
Norms. *See also* Values
patriarchal, 31–32

Oral tradition, 56–57, 91–92,
98–99

Play, ritualized, 100
Playing the dozens, 91–102
ambivalence towards women aspect, 91, 95–96
as coping mechanism, 101–102
definition, 92
origins, 97–99
pornographic aspect, 93–94, 95
rhyming aspect, 95
as ritualized play, 100
as ritualized sexuality, 93–95
Poverty rate, 15
Powell, Adam Clayton Jr., 4
Pregnancy, adolescent, 16–17
infant mortality and, 18
Premature death, 22
Pride, ethnic, 38–39
Psychotherapy, self-disclosure in,
40–41

Race relations, behavioral styles
in, 52–53
Racial awareness workshops,
115–116
Racism
institutionalized, 24, 25
stereotyping and, 24
Rape, 22, 23, 52
Rawls, Lou, 81–82
Reaction formation, 49
Rebellion, 7
Reputation, verbal ability and,
100–101
Retreatism, 6–7
Ribbing, 96
Risk-taking behavior, 19, 21, 30
denial and, 49–50
reaction formation and, 49
Robinson, Bill "Bojangles," 70

Samboism, 7
Schools. *See also* Academic under-
achievement; Education
desegregation of, 114–115
Self-control, 29
Self-destructive behavior, 19
Self-disclosure, 40–41
Self-esteem, 39, 46
Sexual promiscuity, 16–17, 34
Shine, 33
Shucking, 63
Simple, Jesse B., 64–65
Slavery, 58–59, 60, 98, 101
Smoking, 21, 34
Socialization
Afrocentric, 110–113
familial, 49
Social programs, government fund-
ing reductions, 25
Social stress indicators, 11–25
academic underachievement,
12, 13–15
accidental death, 21

About the
Authors

Richard Majors' work on cool pose has received national and international attention. Author of several articles and chapters on African-American males, Majors has appeared on numerous television and radio programs. His work has been cited by *USA Today, New York Times, Chicago Tribune, Chicago Sun Times, Orlando Sentinel, Detroit Free Press, Washington Post, New York Daily News, New York Newsday, Time, American Vision, Jet,* and *Reader's Digest.*

Majors is co-founder and chairman of the National Council of African American Men (NCAAM)—a national umbrella group designed to help shape public policy and legislation affecting black males—and is co-founder and consulting editor of the *Journal of African American Males Studies (JAAMS).*

Born in Ithaca, New York, Majors was an American Psychological Association Predoctoral Minority Fellow Award Recipient in Research. He received his Ph.D. in counseling psychology from the University of Illinois, Urbana-Champaign. After finishing postdoctoral work at the University of Kansas, Majors served as a Clinical Fellow in Psychiatry at Harvard Medical School. He is currently an assistant professor of psychology at the University of Wisconsin, Eau Claire.

Janet Mancini Billson, author of *Strategic Styles: Coping in the Inner City* and *Encountering Society,* has devoted her career to exploring issues of identity for minorities and women. She worked on the respected *Pathways to Identity* project at Harvard University, which studied young black males growing up in the Roxbury section of Boston in the 1960s. She has published and lectured extensively on social change among native people in Canada and is currently writing *Journeys into the Heart,* a book on the impact of culture on gender roles among Canadian women.

Mancini Billson received her Ph.D. in sociology from Brandeis University, where she was a Woodrow Wilson Fellow and a National Institute of Mental Health Field Work Fellow. After many years as professor of sociology and Women's Studies at Rhode Island College, Providence, she is serving as assistant executive officer of the American Sociological Association in Washington, D.C., and as an adjunct professor of sociology at George Washington University. A certified clinical sociologist, she has maintained a private practice in group facilitation training and focus group research.